THE FIRST FIVE TO SEVEN YEARS

THE
The tale of one woman's search
FIRST FIVE
the world over
TO SEVEN
for her highest and best use
YEARS

Emily Kempf

PERDIZES PRESS

Published by Perdizes Press

ISBN 979-8-9881773-0-2

This work depicts actual events in the life of the author as truthfully as recollection permits.

Cover and interior design: KUHN Design Group | kuhndesigngroup.com

Logo design: Garland Studios | garlandstudios.com

To my children, who teach me

1

ZENITH

Impossibly confident and chic, she held the table's attention as effortlessly as she wore her silk scarf. It was not her dinner party, yet she had ruled it from the moment of her arrival. Tilting her head, she gazed at the man in the bespoke blazer to her right and murmured, "So, what do you do?" Candlelight flickered, illuminating misty twilight views of Manhattan's Downtown and Midtown skyline. I held my breath, waiting in nervous anticipation.

The question snaked around the table until the *grande dame* turned to me. I met her commanding gaze. With the gauntlet thrown down, I smartly replied, "I investigate fraud and corruption."

It was such a relief to have this response. This was a social event, but I would be foolish to think I could relax. Living in New York, I could expect my fellow guests to be or become tastemakers, experts, connoisseurs, maestros. This expectation was the rationale behind the otherwise puzzling logic of paying a premium to live one's life squashed. New Yorkers rise in and retire to minuscule apartments, navigate crowded stations and sidewalks, and toil in towers whose upward creation of space was never sufficient. For those playing the city's game, that of becoming someone, the sharpening effect of proximity to the best redeemed these inconveniences. The city's collective expectation of influence, instruction, or inspiration made this standard opener an important ritual. The opportunity cost was simply too high to allow the answer to be pro forma or friendly. When responding, I was always painfully aware of the unspoken evaluation: "Should I bother with this person or move on to the next?" And I desperately wanted to have a winning answer.

When I moved to New York after graduating college, I was an accountant—an answer with which I faded into the obscurity of the evening mist. Even worse, while I was no country bumpkin, I was perhaps perceived as such. I grew up Minnesota Nice and studied at the University of Notre Dame, known for football and turning out brainy do-gooders. I would say things like "dang it," oblivious to how simple I sounded. I was hard working and accustomed to courtesy as the norm that governed interactions. It's how I was raised. Unsurprisingly, my early professional life at an accountancy consultancy showed me to be a good performer, but lacking the social finesse required this far east. In my naïveté, I freely shared stories of my bucolic past: "More people work in this office building than populate my hometown!" Now I was 24 and my room in a shared Upper East Side apartment was not much larger than the stalls that used to house my livestock in Minnesota.

The damage to my reputation had been done by the time I realized my colleagues did not reciprocate with their own charmingly genuine tales. I only learned the full impact of what I had done when my manager brought a small suitcase to the office one Friday. A friendly inquiry into his weekend plans was halfway out of my mouth when his uptight countenance stopped it short; it was as if he were sucking a sour lemon. At that moment I realized the reticence to share personal information arose from a strategy that maintained a strict focus on the real topic: work. And in a culture in which 80-hour weeks were typical, talking about your life might reveal vulnerability and an inadequate commitment to this work. So to get ahead, I would have to drop what I considered to be of interest and good manners—and fast.

While I had expected and could handle the long hours, I struggled to adapt to the invincible show my new environment demanded. I made some rookie mistakes for which my manager showed little patience. Under pressure to meet his own deadlines, he needed his fresh-faced trainees to perform flawlessly and with the efficiency required in the city that coined the term New York minute. With a purse of his lips, a tense tone, or an exasperated sigh he would at once decimate my tender confidence while also redoubling my motivation to achieve the required perfection. Ahead of a review, I would stare hard into the tidy schedules on my computer screen, imploring them to reveal any mistakes I missed in my own cross-examination. When summoned, I would pick up my laptop and walk slowly over to his desk, as if keeping time with the slow beat of an executioner's drum.

A second project showed my first to be no anomaly in its oppressive commitment to work. I spent months cramped in a crowded conference room located two floors below ground, allowing us to hear the rumble of subway trains passing below our feet. Taking the elevator down each morning I imagined myself a miner, bidding farewell to the sun and descending into the depths of the Earth to begin my toil. I would emerge only for a quick lunch or coffee break and again at day's end, long after sunset.

As the deadline approached, I dared not smile since doing so would suggest I was not sufficiently miserable, ergo, in need of more work. One late night after many, the team's closet jokester, probably a touch delirious, risked breaking this unspoken code to print and hang a picture of a window, allowing humorous light to dissipate the room's tension and lingering smell of take-out dinner. Emboldened, the team's other closet personalities, including mine, momentarily emerged to celebrate our colleague's act of rebellion. The window, permitted to remain, hung as a memento of fun's solitary victory before order was restored. I often turned to that "window" to remember the fun. Humor was important to find, especially as the work only became more intense. In the project's final throes, the team's senior manager contracted the highly contagious pink eye, but nevertheless came to work, directing his team from an allegedly safe distance.

From this collective awfulness I emerged a professional with a heightened standard for excellence, aware of the commitment required, and hungry to prove myself in this exhilarating game I now had the savvy to play. Each morning as my No. 4 train lurched into Grand Central Station, I celebrated my hard-earned credibility with a quiet smile. As a newcomer I had been unaware the game was already in play the moment I disembarked, the station so intensely crowded that merely making an exit required strategy and a touch of daring. During my apprenticeship I observed my fellow commuters and learned to combine their bold stride with a "thousand-mile stare," a look that appeared as if my gaze were directed at a distant point but, in reality, perceived all obstacles en route. Now a contender, I stepped out into the crowd, clad for combat in my black trench coat and patent leather heels, ready to play one round of chicken after another in the hopes of emerging first in the shadow of the station's Beaux-Arts exterior. The reward for a fleeting victory was the opportunity to race on again.

Youthful and summoned onward and upward by the dynamic environment, I planned for a future of consequence. I also felt called to use my God-given talents to their highest and best use.

The clarifying power of life's challenges allowed me to discern an exciting trajectory in my pursuit. Late one night in that gloomy, windowless team room, I sat evaluating the choices that had led me to this bunker. I recalled what most intrigued me about my accounting classes was not what I was now doing — routine financial statement audits — but the work of protecting the markets from fraud. My studies occurred in the aftermath of Enron and WorldCom, financial statement scams resulting in billions of dollars in losses and sweeping regulation reform — adding real-life drama to an otherwise humdrum lecture on an accountant's duties of care.

In parallel, I had been using my free weekend hours to read wonkish publications like *Foreign Affairs*, *The End of Poverty*, and *The Bottom Billion* to see where my skills might best fit in the industry of saving the world. I elected to major in accountancy understanding it to be versatile in its applicability and well-suited to my analytical nature, yet public policy also interested me.

Gradually the team room epiphany and my reading fused into a desire to work on fraud and corruption investigations, with the goal of eventually transitioning to the policy world. Exploring professional roles that fit these interests, I discovered my own densely populated Midtown skyscraper housed a world-class investigation team in another department on one of the privileged above-ground floors. I promptly sent my resume and was elated when my transfer went through a few months later.

My new group had the same steely work ethic, but boasted the added benefits of desks in view of real windows, a refreshing dose of camaraderie, and the excitement of exotic travel. I was not with the group long before my projects had me flying to distant locations. Together we were an Excel-wielding SWAT team, just as ready to deploy to another continent as across town. We uncovered misdeeds, preserved evidence, and calmed nervous bystanders. And when the weekend came with plans to visit such attractions as the Taj Mahal, Korean Demilitarized Zone, or Phuket's beaches, I gleefully congratulated myself on the shrewd professional maneuver I had orchestrated to get me there.

My new job description earned me entrée at the dinner party. Yet the anxiety that tinged my relief reminded me achievements could not remain static. The appetizers finished, the host ushered in the next course and topic of conversation. I inhaled and braced myself. The game was always in motion.

2

DEPARTURE

Hello?" I answered groggily, already knowing the caller to be my fiancé Josh, yet less clear about why he might be calling so late.

Josh and I started dating in college after volunteering on the same political campaign. Like me, he hailed from a small town; his family's deep roots in Texas qualified him as a Son of the Texas Republic, a Wild West version of the Daughters of the American Revolution. True to his ancestors' cowboy spirit, he pursued his dreams with a fearless grit. He had insatiable curiosity and similarly felt called to apply his immense talents to doing great things. He also moved to New York after graduation, having landed a coveted investment banking job and a quasi-rent controlled apartment that gave us access a spectacular rooftop space, where we delighted in hosting dinner parties. All the ingredients for an enchanting evening were at hand: the Manhattan cityscapes, an endless supply of fascinating invitees, and a nearby Whole Foods.

That spring Josh had proposed while we were in Brazil on vacation. Even as New Yorkers adhered to an ethos of "work work work," they were experts at making the most of precious free time. We had decided to visit Brazil, intrigued by the country's vibrant, warm culture and because we wanted to round out our South America education by finally visiting its largest country after studying and traveling in many other countries in the region. Brazil did not disappoint. First visiting São Paulo, we discovered a melting pot of people with big dreams, not unlike the social scene we enjoyed in New York. Moving on to Rio de Janeiro, we danced *samba* and sipped *caipiranhas* with vistas of glittering ocean blue speckled by jagged mountain rocks. On the final day of the trip, atop the Corcovado mountain and below the city's iconic *Cristo Redentor* statue, Josh asked me to marry him. As the magic of the trip and proposal evinced, I knew I would always have someone to share the chase for the extraordinary by saying "yes" to Josh. The possibilities of our future seemed as grand and certain as the Corcovado was high and firm. And the outstretched arms of the Cristo gave me comfort that our union was under God's protection and guidance.

Josh and I had been managing a long-distance relationship since the start of summer when he returned to São Paulo to take Portuguese lessons. He had finished his investment banking training program and planned to start graduate school in London in the fall. He decided to use his free summer to learn Portuguese as he was to return to investment banking and cover the Latin American desk after graduate school. Josh and I would reunite in London, where I had recently negotiated with my employer for an international assignment.

I had last seen him while assisting a hurried exodus of his bachelor apartment. An outbound flight already beckoning him, we had frantically packed flatware and candlesticks, treasured mementos from our exhilarating journey into adult and New York life. Haste and the assurance of carefully made plans—the contents of these boxes would soon emerge in a Manhattan apartment of our own following our stint abroad—had allowed only a brief farewell.

His call from Brazil portended a new journey.

"Hey, sorry did I wake you?" Josh apologized.

"Yeah," I mumbled. "What's up?"

"I just came back from drinks with Felipe."

Josh had met Felipe during an investment banking training program at the start of their careers. Felipe returned to the company's São Paulo office after the training, but they had kept in touch over the years.

"Oh?"

"Felipe asked me to join him at a company he recently founded."

Josh had arrived in Brazil in 2011 when it once again was the "Land of the Future" with entrepreneurs descending *en masse*. Responding to the exuberance, Josh had even started a blog interviewing founders to learn more about Brazil's burgeoning startup scene.

"Well, what do you think?" I sleepily responded.

"The potential for an e-commerce startup like his company is incredible. The market is huge and underdeveloped. If trends follow those we've seen in the U.S., first movers will ride a wave of breakout growth. I'm not sure if it makes sense to join Felipe, but I'd like to investigate my options."

He delivered the possibility with a magnetic propulsion I knew to be endearingly characteristic of his response when possibilities piqued his curiosity. I sat up to further awaken and to better meet his enthusiasm. Josh had responded "entrepreneur" in that classic elementary school career assignment, selected St. Homobonus, the patron saint of entrepreneurs, at confirmation. He confided to me among our courtship disclosures that our life together might include the uncertainties of such a life. Seeing his peer and buddy make the leap, his boyhood dream emerged from the hazy realm of "someday" to the forceful reckoning of real possibility.

"Okay. What would this mean for our plan to go to London?"

"Honestly, I'm not sure. What would you think about skipping London and going instead to Brazil?"

"Skip London?!?" I balked reflexively.

He knew I had called more favors than I was entitled to secure this London assignment, which was just over a month away. And he certainly knew I loathed a last-minute change of plan.

"Maybe," he continued unabated. "I wish you could have been there to hear our conversation. Felipe made me see the immense opportunity that is here for the taking right now. I don't know how things will change in a year or two."

I sighed. I saw now the impetus behind this late night chat: the urgent need to respond to an unanticipated, nevertheless pivotal proposal. Should we forgo the lucrative, but predictable benefits of corporate life, including its inviting UK stint, to strike out on our own, chancing Brazil and the opportunities Josh saw there?

"Well, what would I do if we go straight to Brazil?" I grumbled.

"It might be tricky, but I bet you could transfer to the São Paulo office. Or maybe get a job there with a different consultancy?"

I sighed again. I had to admit to myself that beyond its atrocious inconvenience, the possibility was enticing. A tour in the developing world would provide me with coveted "unique experience" to establish myself as a corruption expert. I believed Josh capable of success in any pursuit, and I wanted to be supportive of his dream. It might even be fun; Brazil had made a favorable impression during the visit when we were engaged.

"I agree. It could be exciting. But then again, I just don't know. It's late. Let's talk about it in the morning."

"Ok. I love you."

"Love you, too."

I collapsed under my covers but found a return to sleep impossible. A dizzying merry-go-round of options revolved in my head, shiny fleeting baubles and perilous pitfalls moving at warp speed, all demanding careful consideration in equal measure.

At the office not long after the groggy phone conversation with Josh, I exhaled relief when my co-worker finally turned to leave. I had not yet shared the news of my London assignment with my team, fearing being deemed a waffling opportunist should I have to renege on the plan. And my surviving Midwest affability was ill-suited to the disingenuous "conversation management" that keeping secrets entailed. Even in responding to a co-worker's cheery inquiries about our wedding plans, a topic my paranoid mind flagged as dangerously close to life plans, a squirming discomfort begged me to shout, "We have no idea where we are going to be next month, okay!?!"

I burrowed myself between the two cubicle walls on either side of my office chair, hoping the pale gray paneling would shield me from further human interaction. To avoid it, I stared intently at my computer screen. In my awaiting work I could analyze vast data sets, uncover hidden patterns, and prepare an orderly solution for clients. Yet the mess of my life had proved impervious to such techniques, with recent developments only complicating our decision. Adding possibilities beyond London grad school and São Paulo startup, Josh had scored interviews with a prestigious venture capital fund that would have placed us in Washington, D.C. or San Francisco.

Eclipsing any preference I had for one location over another was a desperate desire to restore the assurance of a plan. In my uneasy state I didn't even have the comfort of action. Stuck in a holding pattern while Josh pursued options, I could only entertain endless hypotheticals. Assessing and reassessing the incomplete information available to me, I grasped for control that was not to be found and thrashed against a wall of uncertainty.

My phone buzzed, signaling a text and interrupting worried thoughts. I looked apprehensively at the screen to read the message:

"So which time zone are you moving to today?"

Thus embraced by the comedic empathy of a good friend, an unwitting smile escaped my best antisocial game face.

I emerged from the Underground, my expression and stride set to meet an onslaught of foot traffic crossing London Bridge. Enjoying a few airy seconds before joining the pulsating pedestrian mass, I admired the slice of England's splendor before me, glimpsing Tower Bridge and the HMS Belfast before looking up to the Shard slicing the bright morning sky. A quiet smile betrayed my satisfaction. Having survived an agonizing deliberation long distance, my fiancé and I were reunited. We had decided to stick with our plan to spend a year in London so we might discern our next move calmly. I had seamlessly assimilated into a team I admired, seeing my co-workers as modeling the best of British stoicism and ingenuity in working to solve the headline-grabbing cases that inevitably fell into their capable hands. And, as the view before me evinced, the grandeurs of Europe were mine to enjoy.

A proper soul myself, I reveled in England's legendary civilizing traditions that permeated normal life: the "get to know you" cup of tea that often commenced even professional relationships, cufflinks as everyday wear, "hear hear" as an affirmative flourish used credibly by all, not only theatrical parliamentarians. The hundreds of colorful boats that cheerily meandered down the Thames in preparation for Queen Elizabeth II's Diamond Jubilee River Pageant, providing me with pleasant distraction one afternoon at work. But, plunging into the crowd, a wave of sadness chased my contented musings. While London had delivered the diverting culture and rigorous training I desired, life abroad had also introduced an unwelcome traveling companion: loneliness. For the first time, significant barriers—a costly international flight and limited vacation days—separated me from the friends and family with whom I had built ties over a lifetime, the communities with whom I had a natural citizenship. While I had readily formed many strong friendships in New York, I struggled to find similar companionship in London.

A casual coffee run revealed a cultural dividing line that contributed to this difference of experience. At Starbucks for an afternoon pick me up, I happened across a promotion that gave free coffee to all customers who shared their names. Long accustomed to telling my name to baristas free of incentive, I thought it a splendid deal. I eagerly conveyed to the cashier, "Hello! I'm Emily." Then moving to the side to await my prize, my attention gravitated back to the cashier.

"Hello! Would you like to share your name for a free cup of coffee?" the barista cheerily asked. The waiting customer, a gentleman in a tweed suit, appeared momentarily confused and then mumbled his name directly into the barista's ear. He joined me in waiting, and the barista sounded off again in her patented cheery tone, "Hello! Would you like to share your name for a free cup of coffee?" This time the customer, a no-nonsense businesswoman, huffed, "What? No, no thank you."

"Emily!" the barista shouted. I looked up with a start. Taking my coffee, I surveyed the scene once more before leaving. "What do they have against free coffee?" I wondered.

Back at the office I asked my co-worker about what I had seen. He explained that some Brits consider a proper introduction necessary to share one's name. I laughed. Prerequisites to share a name? If

I were the only one receiving free coffee in exchange for my name, that was fine with me. I loved a good deal.

Reaching the other side of the bridge, I turned off on the road leading to my office, brushing off my concerns as I rounded the corner. Surely these feelings of loneliness were temporary, only an unfortunate byproduct of local culture. With the winds of change already shifting I had no reason to mope. Josh and I had a wedding to plan and a future to decide.

"Well, I suppose this is our last hurrah for a while," Josh said.

"I suppose so," I replied.

Josh and I had just finished lunch at a charming sidewalk cafe in Nice. Two weeks earlier we were married at the Basilica of St. Mary in Minneapolis. Like many girls, I had decided on key details of my wedding long before ever meeting the groom. The Basilica of St. Mary was not my home parish growing up, but it won my heart for its gorgeous Beaux-Arts design (foreshadowing my affinity for Grand Central Station) and stately presence; its location on the edge of Minneapolis made it the centerpiece of the city's skyline. It was also where I received my sacrament of confirmation, my adult initiation into the life of the faith. I thought it only fitting to return to celebrate my marriage.

Some details a girl can plan, others are a wonderful surprise. The governor danced at our reception; *The New York Times* published our wedding announcement. The meal in Nice, exquisite in its lush freshness, epitomized and ended the gastronomic feast that had been our honeymoon through northern Spain and the French Riviera.

Though the time had come for us to depart, we lingered, savoring the scene and the finality of the moment. In rising we would leave behind security and cosmopolitan comforts, pursuing instead what had become our Brazil dream. If our mountain top, ocean view engagement constituted a mystical pact to relocate and begin a life there, we had been blissfully unaware. Yet during our time in London, Josh had flown back to São Paulo several times, gradually formulating an idea to found, grow, and eventually sell a B2B e-commerce company, thus leveraging the gains of incorporating a massive, unsophisticated market into Brazil's exploding online sector. He estimated such an effort would take five to seven years, after which we could hope to move back to the States, carrying the prize of financial flexibility. Weighing our options, we saw the U.S. still sputtering following the 2008 financial crisis, an event that had overshadowed our debut into the workforce. Two months earlier I had proudly watched Josh leave London for São Paulo to begin work, confident in his plan and encumbered only by two suitcases. Confirming his resolve, he had recently informed his New York boss he would not be returning as planned upon the completion of his graduate degree.

With the decision made to move to Brazil, I had to negotiate my second international assignment in less than a year, relying on my desire to stick with the man I loved and the dream we were chasing to override my embarrassment of the audacity of my demands. Having received positive indications from the São Paulo team, I giddily imagined the content of my future resume: Fraud Investigator: New York, London, and São Paulo.

Timetables again demanded a farewell, interrupting the afternoon torpor. "Well, let's get going then."

"Yep. Let's do this," Josh agreed.

We rose. Flights awaited though our destinations would be far apart: Josh to Brazil and I back to London to finish my assignment before joining him in São Paulo three months later.

3

BEM VINDO

I looked out the taxi window, taking in grim buildings, strewn litter, and the graffiti covering the highway's barricades, shoulders, and overpasses. Motorcycles sped past, the drivers skirting traffic by riding the dividing white line *beep beep beep beeeeeeeping* shrill warnings to cars even thinking about a lane change. The *Tietê* River separated us from oncoming traffic, its murky waters permeating the air with a pungent stench.

Josh had met me at the São Paulo airport earlier that morning, finally commencing our married life geographically united. We headed home — if it could already be called that — accompanied by my two suitcases containing kit carefully chosen for this new adventure. It was my second time in Brazil.

"Um, Emily" Josh started, interrupting my reverie. "I've been asked to pay a bribe to resolve an administrative detail for the company. While a minor matter, it will sink us if we don't resolve it quickly."

Cautionary tales from every corruption case I had worked on and read about filled me with dread. I cried. I had anticipated life in Brazil would expose us to a harsher reality than we previously experienced.

But now? Already? I had passed the long hours of my flight to Brazil contemplating the hard work ahead of building a life. Having the benefit of a solid foundation on which to build, an established relationship and professional track, I was excited about the possibilities. Yet a premonition told me I should prepare myself for anything.

Determined to regain my composure, I returned my focus outside. Having now traveled a ways from the airport, I evaluated each new scene as a possible neighborhood home, silently musing: "Hopefully not there. Maybe there? I guess that street would be okay."

Reality intruded as the taxi came to a stop. "Here we are," Josh announced. Looking out, I saw a shabby-looking building looming above a sidewalk swarmed by pedestrians, storefronts, and precariously hanging telephone lines. I set my face in what I hoped was a positive expression and crossed the threshold of our newlywed home, tear-free. Our nest was a matchbox-sized apartment whose recommending qualities included being furnished, close to public transportation, and free from the troublesome requirement of paperwork we did not have. Once inside, one of my first thoughts was, "I have to buy a towel!" My still bachelor-minded husband had procured only one.

That night I fell asleep to a new crop of worries and the jarring high-pitched labor of city buses struggling up a hill.

Amid morning's hope and energy, I rose ready to work. Unfortunately, I had to reckon with the uncomfortable fact that I did not know what to do. My employment in Brazil with was on hold until I was able to obtain a work visa, which was to come through Josh's company. Josh and I aspired to obtain permanent visas by meeting Brazil's investment requirements. This meant an already lengthy bureaucratic process could not even start until Josh raised some money and hired some people. I had interviewed with the local partners of my consultancy, and they were eager that I start work, but the barrier to entry was on our end. My non-existent Portuguese made me not much help otherwise. Merely buying groceries required me to quell a tempest of doubts. Sizing up the bustling street that led to the store, I worried: "What if I got lost and could not ask for directions?" "Is it even safe for me to walk this road?" "How am I going to carry back all that food anyway? I could take a taxi back, but there again, I would have to communicate."

Hiring a Portuguese tutor was an obvious first step, but not one I was eager for. Ever the conservative accountant, I could not fathom non-discretionary spending when our Statement of Cash Flows mocked me with the distressing red of a negative balance. Covering the next month's rent and groceries looked daunting. I best overcame my fear of going to the grocery store by reminding myself of its potential for economy. I hated cooking, but it sure was a lot cheaper than dining out.

The timeline for the visa that would allow me to work was hazy. Brazilian bureaucracy was notoriously convoluted and slow. Josh had just secured some initial investment and launched a first version of his site, but he had no meaningful or predictable income. Any savings from our short-lived lives of gainful employment had evaporated somewhere between Josh's grad school, European explorations, and our wedding. Even maintaining a hermit's lifestyle would involve burning cash we did not have. Yet my entrepreneurially minded husband insisted I begin Portuguese lessons promptly so I would be ready to work when my visa arrived. Thus, I began spending every morning in the pleasant company of my tutor and every afternoon studying my notes.

A new normal established, I could not escape the nagging sensation that this visa limbo was relegating me to a lady of leisure and a drag on the family finances. Josh would leave for work and I would find myself alone, desperate for productive outlets to funnel the pent-up energy I had stewing. Sequestered in our apartment, the clock was my overlord; every glance in its direction led me to reproach myself for having let so much of the day pass having accomplished so little. I wondered how else I could fill the long hours.

"Enjoy your funemployment! Relax! Explore!" friends would advise. Maintaining that all important "everything is ok here" status quo, I would blithely mumble, "Yeah it is great to have some time off." What else could I say? "Well actually, I'm going a tad crazy as I have almost nothing really to do. Oh, and we are far too broke for relaxation and fun." The way I saw it, fate had cruelly benched me just as the game was getting exciting and my team most needed me. All the while our family finances would free fall until I could get back to work making a difference.

Meanwhile, I could not escape the reality fermenting beneath the surface. My already zealous productivity had gone into hyperdrive faced with an environment that denied it a defined purpose. Facing intractable circumstances, I resolved to add value in the simple activities available to me. When Josh left for work, I would hasten to the corner newsstand, buy a paper, and race home to bag the day's first accomplishment, all before my nerves caught up with me. I sat at my desk and smoothed the pages of the paper, scanning headlines to pick an article to decode. The coming intellectual exercise relaxed me. I set to the task, jotting down vocabulary and tidbits of interest. The notebook scribbles eventually evolved to a nascent understanding of my new home's impotent checks and balances, mishmash legislation, and miscreant politicians who contributed to the evident corruption. I relished my emerging expertise.

I read and reread that Brazilian representatives cast a secret ballot when voting to remove a colleague convicted of corruption. I leaned back in my chair, incredulous to my core that such a blatant abuse of power was legal, but also pleased at having uncovered such an electric insight. One of my hopes in moving to Brazil was that such insights would position me as a corruption expert. Picking up on a few ongoing corruption cases, I began sharing observations from my Twitter account, counting new followers and retweets among the day's modest achievements.

Once a week I permitted myself to read my paper at a local *padaria.* Strictly translated, *padaria* means bakery. Brazil is well-known for its coffee, yet it also boasts an appreciation for fresh bread. A Brazilian bakery showcases this deliciousness and functions as local watering hole. While I dared not speak to anyone beyond stammering out my order—I splurged on a latte and croissant—I did enjoy the people-watching.

Yet the flurry and industry of morning always gave way to the interminable afternoon, bereft of inspiration for more activities to answer the clock's tyranny. Flopping on the couch, I would scan my environment and my brain for distractions or ways to be productive. I often would pop up to race up and down the apartment building's 15-floor spiral staircase.

The evening hours often brought another feeling from which escape was difficult: the loneliness I hoped to have left in London. From this vantage, the bright white walls surrounding me evinced an air of solitary confinement. My sentence seemed set for an unknown duration.

I had tried to make friends. Shortly after relocating, I received an invitation to a party with a guest list that was exclusively expatriate women. Getting ready for the party, I congratulated myself on already falling into the sisterhood I had missed in London. Yet judging by the scant contact I had with these ladies following the event, I can only assume I did not make the sorority cut. I traced my downfall to a discussion of ways in which a dog can travel in the airplane's main cabin, it being unconscionable to leave Fido in cargo. A kind interpretation would classify my performance as that of a disinterested bystander, while a discerning eye would have caught the amusement I was trying to disguise. How could I help it? I was raised by a farmer's daughter. I had seen the extremes of doggy mom mania living in Manhattan. Those experiences had landed me firmly on the side of pets being pets and people being people. I could not pretend otherwise, even to fit in. In hindsight, the party was a valuable lesson on how different groups have drastically different criteria for acceptance. New York needed me to be a star performer. In São Paulo I apparently had to be a dog lover. The criteria may have varied, but rejection smarted across borders.

My alarm rang at 5:30 a.m. and I woke in eager anticipation. The day had finally arrived for Josh and me to leave the confines of São Paulo and explore the jungle that crept up to the city limits.

On the weekends, Josh and I had been exploring our new home with our characteristic rigor. I had learned to travel from my dad, who planned not vacations, but field trips. During such trips, he liked to rise early and buy doughnuts with the hope that a sugar-coated bribe would entice his family out of bed and to the museum right when it opened. As a child, I would pull my covers even tighter, pleading with him, "I will go wherever you want…just please, please, let me sleep until 8:00!" Now, as I traveled as he did, the last laugh was his. Consequently, Josh and I quickly exhausted São Paulo's attractions available to us sans car and resources. Returning to spend our weekends within range of my solitary confinement, I came to understand the city's conventional wisdom: *Paulistanos* wishing to remain sane must regularly get the heck out of town. The city's grind, pollution, and the pervasive concrete made it necessary to escape to Brazil's renowned natural wonders. The city itself used to be a rainforest, with remnants of its past safeguarded just outside our car-less reach.

Fortunately, while riding the metro we happened across an advertisement for a series of day trips run by the city's Transit Authority. The price was modest and it promised a way to leave town—it honestly did not matter where. We promptly registered. Once home, I eagerly awaited our humble day trip in a way I had once looked forward to jetting to Europe or Asia.

An hour later Josh and I were aboard an old train, lurching, rumbling toward the verdant refuge we craved. Soon after arriving, we signed up for a nature hike, confirming with the guide that the tour would finish in time for us to catch our train home. The guide assured us that we would be back in time and off we went. Initially lost in the thrill of fresh air, jungle vistas, and secluded waterfalls, we noticed the hour of our train's departure approaching. Our hike had taken us on a winding path, and we had little idea where we were in relation to our starting point. When we nervously asked our guide about the time, we received a similarly assuring response, and we continued following him. What choice did we have? And what reason did we have to mistrust him? Surely he takes groups on tours all the time and knows how long they last.

When we stopped at yet another waterfall for the group to take one more leisurely dip, alarm bells sounded in our brains' logical command centers, insisting on action. We had one way to get back home: catching our train, the only train that left that day, leaving in some 20 minutes. We approached the guide, did our best to communicate that, while we really were having a lovely time, we thought it best to get going—oh, and would he kindly point the way out of the jungle?

Vaguely confident in our direction of travel, we began a frantic race back down the hill, stopping momentarily once or twice so we could each catch our breath, panting heavily and bracing ourselves with hands on thighs. Fortunately, the conductor caught sight of what must surely have been quite a sight—two foreigners sprinting and waving frenziedly, all while gasping for air. So much for my circular stair training at our apartment building.

Later, when reading an article entitled "Portuguese for the Perplexed" in *The Economist*, I smiled, remembering the reassuring words of our guide up until and including the moment we left him to catch our train.[1] The article offered unofficial translations for foreigners to keep in mind when conversing with Brazilians:

> What Brazilians say: Yes (*Sim*)
>
> What foreigners hear: Yes
>
> What Brazilians mean: Anything from yes to perhaps no
>
> What Brazilians say: Perhaps (*Talvez*)
>
> What foreigners hear: Perhaps
>
> What Brazilians mean: No
>
> What Brazilians say: No (*Não*)
>
> What foreigners hear (on the rare occasion a Brazilian says it): No
>
> What Brazilians mean: Absolutely never, not in a million years, this is the craziest thing I've ever been asked.

Not all the Transit Authority's tours were as eventful, yet all were blessings in that they allowed us to leave the city and return renewed. When we exhausted every available tour, we took to passing free weekend days wandering the city's neighborhoods. The simple apartment buildings, restaurants, coffee shops, and parks we encountered served as a canvas on which we sketched the possibilities of our sure-to-be-happy life in Brazil.

4

INITIATION RITES

"Oi…é Emily….sim, a Americana. Eu gostaria…umm…surgery? Hoje por favor!"

The desperation evident in my voice made up for my middling Portuguese, and the doctor's receptionist put me on hold.

Josh and I had returned from one of our jungle excursions with what we determined were "bug bites." But curiously, they had grown rather than receded. Our lack of local health insurance caused us to avoid seeing a doctor until we felt these "bug bites" move inside us.

"Fly larvae!" the overpriced expat-recommended doctor had gleefully diagnosed. "I haven't seen a case of these in years," he marveled. "We can remove them with a simple operation."

The instant I became aware the "bug bite" atop my head was actually a fly baby, I became increasingly unhinged. I had long harbored a dislike of all God's creatures creepy and crawly, traumatized by early brushes with leeches and ticks in Minnesota's lakes and plains. Yet those were child's play compared to a worm burrowing into my skull, centimeters from my brain. Since I could feel it move, I could not distract myself into temporarily forgetting that I was a parasite host.

Like a little bad angel, prancing on my head instead of my shoulder, the fly baby tormented every activity of my already anxious, mundane life. Reading the paper. Going for groceries. Inventing tasks. Trying to sleep. All were mocked by a "*na-na na-na na nah! You have a bug in your head.*" "Gross! Gross! GROSS!" I would shout, shaking my whole body as if I hoped it would cause the bug to bug out. Compounding my misery, the doctor had postponed my surgery not once, but twice. Placing this call four harrowing days after my diagnosis, the receptionist likely understood she had a simple choice to make: check this poor foreigner into a psych ward or schedule her surgery *pronto*.

The line picked up; "Can you come in an hour?"

I sharply exhaled a gasp of air. (Had I been holding my breath?) "Sim sim!" I nodded vigorously. I swirled into action, grabbing my keys and my phone. I was determined to arrive at the clinic before the doctor changed his mind again. Hours later, I emerged bug-free. Such was my relief that my vanity hardly minded the shaved patch of hair the surgery had necessitated.

The next day I was back in the same bad dream. Josh, having not yet scheduled with our elusive medic, elected to try the local remedy—enticing the larva out by sleeping with a thick, raw slab of bacon atop the wound. His fly baby having made a partial exit by morning, Josh resolved to finish the job with tweezers in the bathroom. Desirous *not* to witness the birth, I retreated to the couch to rock myself back and forth in the fetal position, ruing the day I ever agreed to a life in the tropics.

As if in recognition of our new identities forged by flies, train tours, and other trials since arriving in Brazil, we finally received news that our visas were ready. For nearly a year we had wrangled with the Ministries of Labor and Foreign Affairs to understand the ever-evolving demands for this visa that was always promised for "next month." During this time Josh had laboriously pieced together a company, and I evolved evermore desperate ways to maintain productivity and sanity in my prolonged solitary confinement.

To receive our visas, we had to present a final round of documentation at the U.S. Consulate in Iguazu Falls, Argentina. Protocol required we leave Brazil to present this documentation so we might reenter the country with our new visas. Perceiving our visa appointment as one more trial to survive, foreboding overshadowed final trip preparations. If our appointment were successful, I could start work and arrest our financial death spiral. Yet the scrimmages I had endured with the country's bureaucratic behemoth had taught me simply showing up with the documents listed in the published requirements did not guarantee success. When battling this beast, logic was irrelevant. Maintaining anything less than a posture of cheerful subservience could sabotage the whole operation.

We landed in Argentina with a stack of documents first vetted by our paid consultant and then triple checked by me. Arriving at the consulate to begin our appointment, Josh and I assumed our usual roles in such a situation: he as spokesman and me as master of documents. We were progressing swimmingly until the attendant lobbed a seemingly innocuous question. "How do your parents' names appear on your birth certificates?"

I froze. Panic overcame me. We did not have our birth certificates with us and Brazilian bureaucrats were exacting about how names appear on official records. Problems resulting from this fastidiousness were so prevalent that the U.S. Consulate in São Paulo offered its citizens in a bind official memos to the effect of, "We hereby decree that John Smith is in fact the same person as John Andrew Smith."

One long distance phone call provided Josh the confirmation he needed. However, the only copy of my certificate was securely stored in São Paulo. Calling my brother, who was born at the same hospital, I learned our mom listed her maiden name on his certificate rather than her married name she used in every other situation. Left with no other choice, I had to make an educated guess based on tenuous circumstantial evidence. After completing our appointment, we were told to return the next morning.

The wondrous sights of our subsequent tour of Iguazu Falls, the world's largest waterfall system, could not dissolve into forgetting my worries about the visa. I berated myself for not thinking to pack our birth certificates, which I had no reason to believe would be necessary. But this stress, and all that accumulated over the past year, melted into broad smiles as Josh and I triumphantly exited the consulate the next morning, visas in hand. Our smiles were reminiscent of those we had as we jubilantly made the procession out of the church as newlyweds. Both were unmistakably genuine, emotionally charged, and accompanied by the same thought: "What could stop us now?" Having survived the inaugural trials, we dared ask this question with even more confidence.

Returning to São Paulo, we landed with a thud. The mood had soured on Brazil's prospects and fundraising became an ongoing existential threat to the company. Josh continued to believe his business and the e-commerce industry would grow despite the country's overall tenuous economy, and he worked tirelessly to convince investors of his vision. He went to one pitch meeting after another, wearing Prada loafers with holes in the soles, a worn vestige of his investment banker life.

Double disappointment shrouded my long-awaited employment. One last administrative detail delayed my start date for another two months. And the salary offered, equivalent to what I received as a first year back in New York, was far below expectation. Given the sad state of our family finances and the difficulty of entering a foreign job market, I was obliged to accept the offer.

While our visas bestowed upon us the legal right to pursue our dreams, it was clear we still had much to learn about how to realize them. Following our jungle hike turned sprint, Josh had pulled up São Paulo on Google Earth to see where we had been in relation to our urban home. Seeing that map displaying the city of São Paulo as a gray blob surrounded by a sea of lush green, he marveled at the contrast. Calling me over to look, he mused, "If humans vacated São Paulo today, the jungle would overtake the remnants of the city in no time at all." São Paulo had a population 12.11 million strong (compared to New York's mere 8.6 million), yet the jungle still held power to devour the entirety of the canvas of life in Brazil. This was the first of many observations that would shape our experiences.

Our failure to understand local cultural cues while hiking resulted in our frantic sprint out of the jungle to catch our train. If we wanted to avoid a similar exit from Brazil, we were going to have to expand our skillset. American can-do spirit and New York work ethic were not sufficient enough. The bureaucratic behemoth we confronted for our visas epitomized a broader dysfunctional system, as did the bribe Josh was asked to pay soon after my arrival. Oblivious to this ethos, raw and unruly, we had set about pursuing our goals in the smart, resolute manner in which we had been trained. But in this world, hard work and grit did not necessarily yield a linear output. Winning tactics were often unconventional, requiring a guerrilla mindset.

I had read that Brazilians often rely on the *jeitinho* or "little way" to accomplish tasks, implying circumventing, bending, or breaking social conventions and rules. A lifelong rule follower, I had regarded this factoid as another insight on my road to expertise, but certainly not as a tool to add to my arsenal.

Unbeknownst to me, a chain of events that saw me accomplice to such an act began one morning when I went to make coffee. Before living in Brazil, I had no experience with either a Moka pot coffee maker or the gas stove it required. In the few months I lived in São Paulo, however, I had acquired a taste for this form of preparation and had witnessed Josh order a replacement gas canister.

This particular morning, I discovered the stove had run out of gas. Feeling bullish on my Portuguese proficiency, I braved calling the gas company to order the replacement. To my delight, I successfully arranged a delivery later that day. Unaware of the saga brewing, I congratulated myself on a newcomer's victory.

Later that afternoon the thrill evaporated when I received a call from the doorman informing me he was forbidden from allowing my delivery as management had recently prohibited the use of gas canisters. He explained that the building had switched to providing gas through pipes installed in the walls and that our landlord could tell us more about how to get our particular unit connected to this network.

When Josh finally reached the landlord of our rented unit, he learned she had received the first as well as final notices about the prohibition but disagreed with the building management on required reforms. From her Chicago apartment, where coffee could be made, food prepared and reheated without concern about the availability of fuel, she had decided that this was a battle she wanted to fight. The standoff dragged on for days, then a week and then two. Feeding myself with my elementary cooking skills was hard enough with a working oven and stove; now I struggled to manage with just a microwave at my disposal. While I could have survived eating sandwiches and cereal for days, I pined for a cup of coffee.

Marriage allows for division of labor and in ours, Josh was the resident bad cop and shrewd negotiator. Coffee-less morning after coffee-less morning, I would beseech Josh to find time in his day keeping his company afloat to call and argue with the landlord yet again. Then one afternoon, the ringing of the apartment telephone interrupted my uncaffeinated, uninspired study of irregular verb tenses. Answering, my brain immediately switched to hyper-alert mode so I might hope to make some sense of the everyday vernacular that often seemed like a different language entirely from the formal Portuguese I was attempting to master.

This call featured a male voice and, as best as I could make out, he had something to communicate to me about the gas situation. I assumed it was one of the doormen and after thanking him for the information I barely understood, I resolved to wander down later and ask him to relay the message again. I would employ my now-trademark smile and apology. "I am sorry I'm such a dense foreigner, but would you mind explaining that to me again, a bit slower this time?"

I had just returned to my irregular verbs when I heard a knock at the door. Looking through the peephole, I was surprised to see the older gentleman I recognized as The Crazy Cat Man. In my running of the circular stairs I had observed this man to be the owner of the cats that freely wandered the building. He had observed me to be a well-meaning foreigner with surplus energy. While I firmly believed pets to be pets, I did enjoy petting a kitty every now and then. We had yet to have any conversation given the language barrier, but I had started greeting him with a variant trademark smile: "I'm sorry I can't communicate, but I promise I'm a nice person."

Opening the door, the scene before me both struck me dumb and made my heart leap. The Crazy Cat Man stood before me, rather winded from what I surmised to be him lugging the gas canister that lay at his feet to my door. I pondered one question after another as

I stood there speechless. How did this man, given his advanced age and suspect fitness, manage to haul such a heavy object? How did he know we desperately needed a new canister? And then the question I barely dared to hope—could this be the end of microwave cooking and no coffee?

Breaking the silence, he explained that he had heard of our predicament from the doormen and wanted to help since he happened to have a gas canister stored. Continuing his tale, he glowed with a mischievous pride as he related his hero's tale of telling off the doorman, who had threatened to report him if he helped the poor foreigners. He then nonchalantly offered to install it for me.

Still dumbfounded, I hardly knew what words I managed to string together as I ushered him to the minuscule laundry room of my matchbox apartment so he might install the canister. While he set about to perform yet another superhuman feat, lifting and adjusting the heavy canister into position in a space comically small in proportion to his considerable size, I stood back observing, awash with overwhelming gratitude. Completing his task, he accepted my profuse thanks and then left without ceremony.

Reflecting over a celebratory coffee, I realized that the afternoon's covert operation was *jeitinho* at work. I treasured the incident as my true initiation into life in Brazil. Unbeknownst to me, smiles and stair running had made me a member of the community worth chancing superhuman feats and the wrath of the building administration. Piping mug in hand and warm thoughts on my mind, I felt a little more at home.

5

MASTER'S IN *MERDA*

Half-asleep late one evening when Josh came home from work, I forgot to ask him about his day. Instead, he announced the news that could not have waited until morning: "I saved a man's life today." His message was delivered as a matter of fact, without fanfare. It was only when my tired brain processed the jarring implications of his message that I fully awoke. My shock contrasting his apparent aloofness, I demanded the story.

"It all started when one of my employees came back from a smoke break screaming. I ran outside to find blood dripping down the spiral staircase of the guard tower. My security guard had shot himself in the thigh while playing with his gun. My first thought was that he was done for. Blood was gushing everywhere and I knew there was an artery around there. I used his belt to make a tourniquet, but then had to use mine after his snapped."

I noticed his sagging pants that were missing the belt he had meticulously selected to match his loafers. I was in awe of his aplomb and the combined Boy Scout and lifeguard first aid he was able to revive after all these years.

"The hardest part was getting the man down the stairs. He is a big guy so I couldn't carry him and he couldn't put any weight on his injured leg. After getting him down the stairs, I loaded him in the company car, putting a tarp down first, and sped off to the nearest public hospital."

I searched his face for a flicker of panic or fear, but found none. He continued his story in the same unexcited way as he had begun.

"When I arrived at the hospital, I had trouble getting anyone's attention. I had been worried about explaining why I had a gunshot wound victim in my car, but nobody seemed to bother about that or anything else. I had to run around until I finally found someone who would attend to him. I basically had to threaten, '*This man is going to die unless you help him now!*'"

He finished his story on an upbeat note. "I spoke with his supervisor just now and his condition is stable."

Exhaling with the dramatic close, I wanted to scream, "How is this the type of news that waits for the end of the day?!?" In my world, my family, friends, neighbors, the mailman, a handful of acquaintances, and perhaps a few complete strangers would have all heard this tale of blood and danger well before nightfall. Instead, I asked in feigned nonchalance, "So, why did you wait until now to tell me?"

Silence. Then he said, "Most days I feel like all I do is put out fires."

I knew it was true, figuratively and literally. Previously, the rat's nest of telephone wires at his office caught fire, and he had put it out himself after getting a busy signal at the fire department. No wonder he did not bother calling an ambulance for the wounded guard. I turned the events of the day over and over in my mind. In New York, Josh's desk featured individualized temperature control, a First World extravagance. In Brazil, he was CEO in addition to ad hoc fireman and paramedic. What would I have done had I been in Josh's place? Would the man have survived? Or worse, what if I had been in the place of the hapless security guard, at the mercy of a lackadaisical public hospital?

At the consultancy where I had recently resumed employment, I, too, encountered new environmental challenges—albeit less existential in nature. My day usually began with a hunt for the least broken chair in the office, with latecomers doomed to an annoying inability to see the world straight on or to sit straight up as they worked.

Our morning game of musical chairs proved an apt opening ritual to a day spent making the best of scarce resources. Not long after I started the job, my boss assigned me to conduct investigative interviews, a task I accepted with an astonishment I attempted to conceal. In New York and London, a deep bench of senior staff ensured such a delicate task never reached my level. Never mind I would be holding the interviews in a language I was still mastering.

Determined to succeed, I made extensive notes and rehearsed tongue-twister words I anticipated using. Still, the steady beat of an executioner's drum was once again my soundtrack as I arrived at the client site for interviews. Despite my preparation, I never could seem to muster confidence in such moments, tormented instead by a swarm of angry stomach butterflies. When the interview time finally arrived, I swallowed hard, took my spot at the head of the table with my best "International Fraud Investigator" game face, and plodded mechanically through my prepared questions. Finally closing my laptop—with no one having stood up to point a finger at me and shout, "No, you are the fraud!"—I internally rejoiced. The nearly a year I had spent funneling my nervous energy into Portuguese proficiency and Brazilian current events paid off. I had obtained the information required. Now at the start of my second year Brazil, I was seemingly vetted for an environment that would allow me as much responsibility as I could handle. Unlike my first year, I doubted I would lack for productive outlets.

But I couldn't extinguish my doubts. My nagging subconscious whispered, or sometimes even yelled, "You don't have what it takes." True, I was conscientious, not cunning. A Minnesota girl with a New York sheen. My biggest *jeitinho* foray so far involved opening the door to allow a neighbor to lend me the equivalent of a cup of sugar. Even if I arrived at work in time for one of the good chairs, cultural and communication barriers prevented me from ever engaging this world straight on, as I normally would have. And in this world the fire department sometimes let its phones ring. Intimately attuned to the stakes and the risks, I did not want to get burned.

Explicit in our goals in moving to Brazil—to take advantage of an unsophisticated ecommerce market and to gain unique corruption insights—was contact with a world raw and unruly. Yet in a naïve oversight, we had not considered how it would affect our lives at blood and coffee level. Our second year into the fight, this experiential education that was proving to be a master's in *merda* (sh*t), was the only competitive advantage we had on our peers we left in New York. We had witnessed and wrestled with the country's maddening public services. We sympathized with the many Brazilians, who like Josh's security guard, had no recourse but a woefully inadequate public health system that the World Health Organization ranked in the bottom 35% internationally.[2] And a pervasive culture of bureaucratic stagnation had driven even me, a self-professed rule follower, to embrace the *jeitinho* to gain access to necessities.

In this world, coping mechanisms varied by resources available. Still no one was immune from jungle rule. The country's omnipresent walls, gates, and guards created bastions of security, yet only a fool would consider his or her wallet, watch, or phone safe on the surrounding sidewalks. São Paulo had the world's highest usage of helitaxis to skirt its notorious traffic, but those passengers still landed to breathe the congestion's polluted air to which their luxurious travel contributed. That stench coming from the *Tietê* river? I learned it had been just over a decade since the city began processing sewage rather than dumping it directly into the river. Brazil, after all, only shed its dictatorship and took up the challenges of democracy in 1985, the year before I was born. Planted in this rocky terrain, the stress of what Josh and I had not achieved since leaving New York was ever-present as evidenced by our pathetic family finances and the still-wobbly startup. Like many entrepreneurs, Josh had accepted a modest salary in exchange for a larger share of the company, wagering that its value would handsomely materialize in a future sale.

Our triumphant "What could stop us now?" smiles from the day we finally secured our visas had long since faded. Our belief that intellect and industry invariably yield results was shaken, leaving us with only hustle and an iron resolve to break through the jungle underbrush and grab what we set out to accomplish. I faced the *merda* relying on a notion many Catholics were taught. "Offering it up," enduring my suffering, might count for something. On the precipice of another long day, I would pray the rosary for strength to meet its challenges. I dared not contemplate that we might not someday, somehow break through. Or that our current trials could harm us, ruin us, even devour us. There just had to be another side.

6

DISILLUSION

I rose nervously from my chair when my boss signaled he was ready to accompany me to our next meeting. I knew our short walk would be my best and, perhaps, only chance to broach the topic of my upcoming vacation. Previously, he had suggested I might have to postpone since it coincided with the deadline recently set for our project. There was extraordinary pressure to meet the deadline. And there couldn't have been a bigger, more critical project for our company.

After a six-month delay, we were finally preparing to release the audited financial statements of Petrobras. It was a semi-public oil company with the government as its largest stakeholder. It was also Brazil's largest company and prized corporate jewel. Throughout the delay, Petrobras had been without access to the public debt markets, threatening its solvency and worrying market watchers.

The standoff began when a federal investigation released an explosive plea bargain testimony provided by a former Petrobras executive that shed a mega-watt spotlight on a decade of suspected—but never confirmed—unscrupulous dealings between the country's political parties and Petrobras. The witness detailed a scheme in which

Petrobras executives paid inflated prices on contracts with a cartel of companies in exchange for kickbacks into their personal accounts and those of their political overlords. This testimony transformed a simple money laundering investigation into the largest corruption scandal in Latin America, implicating the country's business and political elite. In a region more accustomed to impunity than an even application of justice, Brazilians celebrated the skillful, humble man leading the case, Judge Sérgio Moro.

The aftermath of the testimony's seismic shock waves included my hasty dispatch to Rio de Janeiro when the Petrobras audit partner requested backup. While Petrobras would later hire an army of outside consultants and counsel, that October morning a co-worker and I were the first external investigators to arrive on the scene. The audit partner met us for a breakfast briefing, closing his remarks with a solemn, somewhat ominous sounding pronouncement. "This will be the most important case you ever work on."

Given the gravity of accusations and the exceedingly public nature of the case, the audit partner had notified Petrobras that he would not sign off on audited financial statements until a further investigation could be made. In turn, he had to answer the natural follow-up question; "What do you need to know to make you happy?" It was a question fraught with risk at both ends of the spectrum. Demanding too much assurance and delaying too long could trigger far-reaching economic turmoil for Brazil's largest company, while requiring too little could result in lawsuits from investors claiming to be misled. As the fraud specialists, we had to help the audit team answer this delicate question.

My co-worker and I spent the next few days poring over investigative reports, allegedly crooked contracts, and available public testimonies. Given the sheer scale, complexity, and importance of the case, we were not surprised to see ourselves returning to Rio de Janeiro the following week, this time accompanied by a full team. This commenced what would be our new normal for the next six months.

While in Rio de Janeiro, our team started the day with breakfast at our Copacabana hotel. We wore stiff, dark suits, attire comically somber next to those dressed far more breezily, as if for a day at Brazil's iconic beach. After our *café*, the workday started in the taxi with the radio invariably blaring news, analysis, or satire related to our project. I would always look out the window to find the *Cristo Redentor* statue and look at it as long as I could, summoning the strength of my faith—as well as memories of a more carefree time and an engagement.

As we left sand and the ocean blue behind, our destination, the Petrobras headquarters, loomed into view. Constructed in the brutalist style, it cut an imposing figure. When walking in I could never escape the feeling that I was marching into the proverbial belly of the beast. I'd wonder, "What fresh horror would the day bring and would I be up to it?"

Tasked with understanding a still unraveling case of monumental proportions, we immersed ourselves in a world of dark dealings. Befittingly, my place of work once again was a windowless room, adding to the belly of the beast feel. At day's end, our team gathered in the audit room to share findings, a discussion that often ended by fading to a depressed silence. Inundating ourselves in the scheme's details—its scope, sophistication, and staggering sums—we had no choice but to face the sheer magnitude of the injustice. Petrobras was founded in the 1950's as a state-owned entity with the mantra "The Oil Is Ours." Its aim was to ensure the Brazilian people benefited from the bounty of their country's natural resources. At the time of our investigation, the state was still a majority shareholder. Thus, the Brazilian people, who had a lawful right to and dire need of this pilfered patrimony, were the victims looming behind our work, and we mourned for them. The oil was theirs.

After months of intense investigative work, the audit partner was finally ready to sign off on Petrobras' audited financial statements the following week. The same week I had long planned to take off to spend with my visiting cousin. Waiting for the elevator, I abruptly embarked on the spiel I had been mentally rehearsing: "I just want to confirm I'll be able to take my upcoming vacation. I am running out of energy, and I just don't think that is healthy given my current situation."

I was pregnant.

For weeks I had felt that familiar pre-deadline sensation of running on adrenaline, and on empty. Long hours plus early and late flights had left me exhausted. I knew the protocol my work culture demanded—power through. My industrious core, which had long governed my actions, propelled me to trudge alongside my coworkers even as I approached burnout. But this time, there was the quiet voice of my nascent maternal instinct demanding, "You need rest—now!" At first, I did not want to listen. Too long I had been trained to think that requesting a lighter load was anathema. My maternal instinct persisted. Then I reasoned, "Well, if it were just me, I would keep working. But it is not just me. I have a responsibility to my baby." Resolved, I knew a knockout punch delivery was required to achieve my aim. I had to make a shocking admission of vulnerability. As much as it pained me, I had to admit, "I cannot."

Pregnancy had only added physical fatigue to a mental unraveling long in the works and slow to reveal itself. I had learned well the lessons of my New York education: excellence requires a workaholic's commitment and hidden smiles. Throughout my professional life, I had suppressed my jovial, curious side, projecting instead an assured invincibility. Maintaining two personalities is exhausting. With part of me always hidden, I never felt as if I were making the best use of my talents.

My wildest dreams could not have produced a more exciting project than my current one, yet it gave me little satisfaction. I was on track for promotion, but despite potential movement up the company ladder, I still felt myself a cog, far from making the difference I had hoped. The experience I had accumulated had yet to provide me with a clever new idea on how to reduce corruption's pernicious effects. Becoming a respected corruption expert would likely involve another decade of consuming Vitamin D-depriving toil. I wanted out.

I had little idea what other jobs I could find; the challenges of finding one in a foreign market remained. But I knew it could not be what I was doing now. If I returned to my job after maternity leave, I could expect to continue commuting to Rio de Janeiro and pay half my meager salary to a nanny. My lofty career aspirations humbled, I just wanted to find a part-time job that allowed us to pay the bills. I had always known that having a baby would drastically reorient my priorities, and I looked to motherhood with the hope of a fresh start.

In motherhood, I also saw the opportunity to build a tribe of my own to cherish. Loneliness had persisted throughout my life abroad. Josh and I found Brazilians extremely friendly, but difficult to count as friends. We joked that our Brazilian acquaintances always seemed to have the scheduling conflict of a niece's birthday party. Besides, I felt myself an inarticulate nincompoop when speaking Portuguese. Joke punchlines would fail to translate. After gathering the courage for a multi-part discourse, I would blank on the vocabulary or correct verb tense. Trying to befriend other expats felt an awful lot like dating—I learned to ask for the check when asked, "So, do you have a dog?" I missed the intimacy of my "pajama friends" as I thought of them, people I allow to see me in my pajamas. Nearly three years into my Brazilian sojourn, all those meeting this qualification were still an international flight away. This loneliness made me treasure the rare opportunities I had to spend time with family and friends.

These two powerful forces, my professional unraveling and an intensifying familial devotion, were determined to go on vacation. I shifted my weight waiting for my boss' reply.

"I suppose you can go."

The following week I logged into spotty wi-fi from my hotel on Ilha Grande, an island off the coast of Rio de Janeiro state, to learn that Petrobras had released its audited financial statements reporting $2.1 billion in bribes and reducing the value of its asset by $17 billion because of corruption.[3] Relieved, I waddled back down to the beach, leaving my final investigative project behind. Ahead was motherhood.

7

BABY BLUES

Returning to São Paulo full-time after the Petrobras project, I found pregnancy integrated me into my community in wonderful new ways. Before taking maternity leave, my co-workers made a show of suggesting they wanted to keep an elevator held on our floor so they could rush me to the hospital as needed. Grandmotherly figures readily fawned over my growing belly, excited by my impending motherhood. Waiting in lines, a national pastime, no longer required supreme patience since I was either ushered to the front or had access to the federally mandated "priority line." Rice and beans, a celebrated Brazilian staple, proved uniquely capable of satiating my ravenous pregnancy appetite. It became an indispensable part of my diet.

Yet Brazil's predilection for Cesarean births, its rates among the highest in the world, was a source of stress. I learned that the lower class considered it the safest way to deal with the inadequacies of public hospitals; a doctor would be more likely to provide his or her full attention for a succinct procedure than a protracted natural labor. And the upper class often viewed it as a more advanced way of giving birth. A typical birth might be preceded by hair and makeup at the in-hospital salon and followed by an afterparty with waiting family members — the post-birth tummy tuck an optional add-on. Also different from the U.S., women insist their specific doctor oversees their birth. The varying quality and methodology of local doctors made relying on whichever one was "on call" an approach to be avoided.

Attempting to navigate this cultural divide, I felt ever the odd woman out. When I called around to different clinics, one receptionist advised me to look for a midwife and another referred me to an activist organization of Brazilians concerned about the predominance of C-sections. I bemoaned, "I don't want a home birth or a cause! I just want to give myself the best chance at a normal birth!"

The relief I had found in an obstetrician who championed normal birth evaporated when, late in my second trimester, I learned our insurance plan made his out of network fees financially untenable. My first-time pregnancy jitters escalated to panic. I fixated on reestablishing the relative calm of an acceptable birth plan and set out to find an in-network provider post haste. Lacking any recommendation, I focused on finding a provider with an office in one of the city's nicer neighborhoods, ideally one who could see me ASAP. I found one and made an appointment. So far, so good.

The day of my appointment came. I checked in with the front desk and then plopped down in a chair in the waiting room. Josh sat next to me and turned his attention to his phone and his still-spinning workday. I looked around for clues of what to expect. I saw that our bench-style chairs were the same as those at the city's bus station. Above them hung warm, generic paintings typical of a well-meaning doctor's office. Taking this all in, I silently calibrated my expectations for a humble, but adequate, path forward.

Then a scene unfolded by the bathroom. Another expectant mother struggled to fit her belly through the space provided by a door, which an uneven floor prevented from opening completely. I was at first incredulous then outraged. I fumed, "If this office cannot even allow pregnant women to pee, how can I trust them with my birth?" Dejected by an uneven floor, I seethed with indignation and looked around for additional offenses.

The struggling woman finally breached the bathroom door and disappeared. My name was called, and I entered the examination room with Josh.

The doctor listened to our concerns, then explained that even in-network his reimbursement from our insurance company was so low he charged an additional fee for normal births. With unexpected and disconcerting candor, he added, "I can complete multiple C-sections in the time it takes me to oversee one normal birth."

Sensing that we could be headed toward an untenable situation, Josh threw himself into the insurance breech. "I spoke to the insurance company, and they said if we arrive at an in-network hospital and an on-staff doctor assesses you are in need of emergency attention, as would be the case in active labor, then subsequent procedures would be covered by our plan."

Josh related his intelligence with a guarded man's pride at a problem solved. He knew he had found the most viable solution to our dilemma, yet he knew me well enough to know I would not like it. Quite right. I summarily determined his report to be a load of poppycock insurance jargon and countered, "How do you know they aren't just telling you what you want to hear?"

I had not forgotten the lessons of our jungle hike; here "yes" could just as easily mean "no." And in the hours I had logged previously with our insurance company, trying to ferret out the particulars of our plan, I had found certainty to be an elusive commodity. Merely registering my foreign name at the beginning of the call would invariably fluster the representative—a kerfuffle from which we would not recover. My attempts to keep it simple—"So I go to the hospital. Have a baby. Then what do we do with the bill?"—only sowed more confusion. Having starred as the confused foreigner many times before, the futility of my calls was no surprise. Expat life had taught me that every society has a unique way of functioning which its inhabitants absorb over a lifetime, creating a vital body of knowledge that residents hardly know they have. The hapless representatives who fielded my calls often implicitly knew the information I was desperately trying to ascertain. And they rarely even considered going the extra mile to educate me, assuming they even could.

Trying his best to sound reassuring, Josh said, "I asked them every way I could think of."

"Okay. How do you know the hospitals operate in this way? We know the norm is to have your dedicated obstetrician oversee the birth."

With actual worst-case scenarios (A non-responsive fire department anyone? How about a nice belt for a tourniquet?), in recent memory, it was not hard to imagine I would be left unaided. Besides, tricking our miserly insurance company to cover the expense they had declined to cover in every other scenario surely required a *jeitinho* acumen beyond our capabilities.

"These are dedicated maternity hospitals. I'm sure they will have the staff and infrastructure necessary," Josh said. Opposites attract they say; Josh, ever the risk-tolerant entrepreneur to my conservative accountant, was satisfied with his solution.

"So you propose I just show up at a hospital when I'm in active labor, with no one in particular expecting me, and trust that I will be taken care of?"

"I think it is the best option."

I slouched in defeat. Far from optimizing my chances at a normal birth, I would be leaving my fate to chance. The familial matriarchs—my mom, grandmas, and aunts—I had spoken with had blithely suggested having faith that all would work out. While they were all women whose faith I admired, faith isn't what I wanted at that moment. If not air-tight assurance, I wanted at least confirmation that I would be admitted to the hospital and have a waiting doctor. Yet I knew we had exhausted our options and that my looming due date demanded we settle on a plan. Helpless to control my circumstances, I settled into an uneasy final wait.

I sat nestled on the couch, book in hand and mug perched in the crook of my massive tummy. An enthusiastic round of baby kicks occasionally interrupted my reading, a display at which I never ceased to marvel. Engaged by pleasant distraction, I could best rest. Left alone, my thoughts were liable to wander back to my many worries.

I heard the door open and Josh came in. He arrived late and battle-worn as usual.

"Hey, how was your day?"

"Not good. My investors called off the deal. They got spooked with today's news of Brazil losing its investment grade credit rating. Then I called the other investor, my only backup option, and they were no longer interested."

I sighed. I knew this story. Twice already in its short history, the company had been weeks away from bankruptcy. While the company was showing promising growth, finding the investor funding to keep it afloat had always been challenging. Recently, Brazil had entered its worst recession since the Great Depression, making the task near impossible. Josh described the associated stress as the weight of an 18-wheeler sitting on his chest.

"I know. It was a dream fundraising scenario."

"Now what?"

"Our only option left is for our existing investors to bail us out with an emergency round."

The influx of expats had already slowed when we arrived three years earlier as Brazil showed the first signs of an economic downturn. Now almost every day brought news of another departure.

"So are we going, too?"

"We'll see. We may have no choice. What do you think?"

My current slate of worries included an outbreak of dengue fever, credible threats of city-wide water rationing, and spontaneous protests producing paralyzing traffic by my Hail Mary pass hospital. And yet I still could not say I was ready to quit. I had invested three years of stress, financial freewheeling, and loneliness. I wanted it all to count for something.

"I think we should stay. Whatever happens, we need to know we gave it our very best shot."

"Okay. I agree. We'll keep at it."

We determined to double down if possible. So I shuffled off to bed, hoping to wake up to a better tomorrow.

8

STAMPEDE

I was certainly feeling a bit off, but having never been in labor before, I was not sure if this was it. I had just finished dinner and a comprehensive biography of Harry S. Truman (as good a way as any to pass the eternal hours that comprise any day past one's due date). With nothing else to do, I settled into the couch and awaited the unknown. Soon after, Josh arrived home and made himself a dinner that my voracious pregnancy appetite considered a cute snack.

Around midnight I was fairly confident what I was feeling constituted contractions. But Josh, tasked with the usual expectant father job of tracking duration and frequency of these pains, chose to demonstrate the seriousness with which he took his responsibility by adopting the role of a skeptic.

"Are you sure that was a contraction? It didn't look like it hurt that bad."

In calmer times we had agreed it would make sense to do as much labor at home as possible to improve our chances of having a normal birth. Loath to leave for the hospital before reaching the threshold of a contraction every four to five-minutes, he was not going to count willy nilly.

"Yes." Inhale...Exhale..."Count it!"

His disbelief infuriated me. I was in pain, terrified of the coming ordeal, and doubtful of my ability to meet its challenges. I wanted to relocate to the supervision of medical professionals ASAP! And what did he know about contractions, anyway? He had as much credibility as he would have had asking, "Emily, is that really how you apply lipstick?" Under normal circumstances I would have wasted time arguing, but labor had endowed me with a preternatural ingenuity allowing me to adopt a far more effective tactic—I flopped. In a performance that would have earned me the respect of the Brazil Football Confederation, I added extra huffs and grimaces to the natural pain I was feeling, just to ensure a favorable ruling. Never suspecting his wife of such guile, Josh responded as expected.

I dressed in hyper-mission mode for the trip to the hospital. It was a chilly night, and I made no allowances for vanity. I selected Josh's college hoodie, sweats, socks, and my new "mom shoes," silver Birkenstocks. By 3 a.m., Josh and I agreed we should leave for the hospital.

After hitting every red light and contraction-exasperating pothole, we arrived at the hospital in the middle of the night stillness. Bursting through the doors, the bright, sterile light flooding the lobby momentarily disorientated me. My eyes adjusted and I spotted the front desk. I charged toward it with the intensity and grace of a stampeding elephant. I was a woman on a mission to receive immediate cooperation with bringing our child into the world.

My frenzied approach was interrupted by a momentary sense of calm that came when I caught sight of a statue of the Blessed Mother, serenely smiling, welcoming me to the place of my own sacred rite of passage to motherhood. I smiled back between the pain, whispering "You got my back, right?" and then tore onward.

My advance came to an abrupt halt when I arrived at the front desk. The rage brought on by what followed undoubtedly added at least a centimeter of dilation.

The security guard calmly directed my attention to a sight familiar in Brazil, but one I despised—the dreaded take-a-number machine.

Seeing my condition, the security guard attempted to take a number on my behalf, but the machine was out of paper.

The security guard summoned someone over to painstakingly replace the blasted roll of paper. The blasted machine became ready for use.

Astonishingly unaware of my presence, a perfectly coiffed, styled, and by all appearances not-in-active-labor pregnant woman darted in front of me to take her number first. Josh forcibly restrained me, encouraging me to work on my breathing exercises and ignore my murderous thoughts.

I took a number and began an agonizing wait for triage. While waiting, I huffed and grimaced around the lobby. On the periphery of my consciousness, at that point principally consumed by pain, I was embarrassed. Why was it always me? The different one. The sole laboring elephant stomping about. I was in the waiting room of a maternity ward; where were all the other elephants? And *why* did I decide to wear socks *with* sandals? Big fuzzy thermal socks and metallic sandals. My name was finally called and we relocated to an examination room to meet Dr. Luck-of-the-Draw. Completing his examination, our newly assigned obstetrician advised, "The baby's heart rate is a bit low. You should consider a C-section."

A C-section?! I was incensed. In my considerable investigation of this practice in Brazil, I had heard that doctors often offered a semi-valid medical reason to encourage C-sections. No way was I falling for it. Had I not been writhing in pain, I would have snarled, "I'm pretty sure I would have skipped out on the last four hours had I wanted to have a C-section!" Alas, I was not in a condition where I could form coherent speech, much less in a foreign language. Instead, Josh coolly, firmly responded, "It is important to us if at all possible to have a normal birth." The readiness in which the doctor accepted our request confirmed my suspicions; my baby was just fine, thank you very much.

I was then wheeled away to the birthing room and Josh was whisked away to scrub in — a standard procedure for all dads given the country's prevalence of C-sections. Contrasting the previous buzz of activity, I now found myself alone except for the presence of a nurse who was infuriatingly doing nothing to ease my suffering or assist in my labor, committed only to her crucial task of methodically stocking cabinets. Now genuine in my flopping, I alternated moaning "Where is my husband?" and "Drugs please!" at the impervious nurse.

After what seemed like an eternity, Josh returned along with the medical team. The buzz of activity recommenced. An anesthesiologist finally arrived and medicated relief flooded my weary body. Still not dilated to a point at which we could push, we were advised to try and rest. Happy to oblige, I had no sooner closed my eyes when I heard Josh meekly inquire, "Would it be possible to go to the cafeteria to get something to eat?"

Josh had eaten a bird-sized dinner, had been up all night, and was not benefiting from the extraordinary adrenaline of a woman in labor. I realized he was about to pass out. The suddenly engaged nurse sternly warned, "You would have to scrub in all over again."

Josh chose to remain. While he was not afraid of the nurse, he was wise enough to recognize that his wife would not take kindly to abandonment again. Catching his eye, I smiled knowingly, saying, "I have a Snickers bar."

A week earlier Josh had noticed this 488 calorie, chocolaty treat innocently nestled in my hospital bag and had made quite a show poking fun at it. Having just spent most of the past nine months in varying degrees of starving, I stood confidently by my choice. Along with Brazil's signature rice and beans, it possessed a special ability to make the hole in my stomach abate. My cousin (a medical doctor mind you) had enlightened me as to their power on our beach vacation months earlier, having packed them with specific intent of caring for her pregnant charge.

Josh smiled sheepishly and I magnanimously handed him my sole emergency snack. (And that, my dear children, is how your daddy avoided fainting during the birth of your brother.)

A few hours later, the doctor advised it was time to push. I assumed the recommended position and pushed with all my maternal brute strength. Revived, Josh enthusiastically darted between being by my side and monitoring progress on the other end. At 10:05 in the morning, after 10 hours in labor, my little kickboxer with the allegedly low heart rate was born in fighting form. Taking my babe onto my chest, I smiled. He wailed. I gazed into his little face—red, scrunched up from crying, wrinkled—and inhaled the wondrous, surreal sensation of finally holding a baby that had long been in my heart.

True to form on momentous occasions, I giggled. Josh shed a few tears. Taking his turn with the baby, Josh came to what he later described as a strangely primal realization that he did not know the baby and the baby did not know him. Thus inspired, he introduced himself; "Hi, I'm Daddy and you're Nicolas."

9

MOMMY!

I looked at Nicolas nestled in his car seat, overcome by how impossibly small he looked next to the towering buildings visible outside the car windows. Having just emerged from our hospital cocoon, I saw the familiar bustle and grime of São Paulo's main thoroughfare, Avenida Paulista, as if in a harsh, augmented reality. A daunting realization loomed as large as the city skyscrapers—my baby and I were now out in the world to fend for ourselves.

For the past five days I had been under the supervision of an army of cheery, no-nonsense nurses whose presence meant I could assure Nicolas' well-being and mine simply by being a good soldier. Nurses would stop by my room at all hours of the day and night, knocking on the door and issuing me orders.

Knock knock... "I'm going to help you go to the bathroom, and then I am going to help you take a shower."

Knock knock... "It is time for you to take this medicine, and I'm going to check your vitals."

Knock knock... "Wake up! It is time for you to feed your baby. Let me show you how."

Knock knock..."I will bathe your baby now. Pay close attention so you learn."

Knock knock..."It is time for you to eat. Oh, and drink this laxative."

Knock knock..."I'm taking your baby to see the pediatrician now."

Knock knock..."I'm here to change your baby's diaper."

And before I knew it, we had cycled right back to "Wake up! It is time for you to feed your baby. Let me show you how."

The visits were endless. Yet I willingly yielded to this central command; I was exhausted and navigating wildly unknown territory. During pregnancy a majority of my emotional and mental bandwidth had focused on the birth. I had taken a newborn class at the hospital which left me feeling like I had been certified for a moon launch following only a breezy pass through NASA's instruction manual. While fake-soothing a doll in class, I concluded it was just one of the challenges I would figure out when I got there. Now there, I was glad not to be in charge. Sure, I did not really want help using the bathroom or taking a shower—but it was a tradeoff I was willing to make.

Naturally I had fretted over what must be the exorbitant cost of my private room, each visiting specialist, and all the diapers and baths the nurses insisted on handling. I was familiar only with the cursory, rudimentary hospital stays common in the U.S. Our time at this "baby resort" had been completely out of the scope of my health insurance due diligence—a complete expat blind spot. I had no idea what our insurance would cover. Had I been able to muster sufficient brain power to chat with my friends at the insurance company, a *knock knock* from a nurse surely would have truncated the call. Moreover, I neither dared nor desired to argue with my well-meaning but insistent taskmasters. Inertia took hold and, in between napping and following orders, I happily basked in the intoxicating joy a newborn brings.

When orders came to mobilize for departure, I held my baby and my breath as Josh marched off to the hospital's administration office to settle our accounts. I could not believe when he emerged reporting our only charge was a small expense related to a piece of equipment used in the birthing room. As it turned out, the prevalence of Cesarean births in Brazil for once worked to my advantage. Women who receive an incision in their abdomen certainly require a multi-day "we'll even change every diaper for you" hospital stay and thus, it was apparently standard for all. What a relief it was to have something I had yet had the chance to worry about turn out not to be a problem at all! Josh and I shared a moment of happy disbelief and then moved quickly to the parking lot.

We loaded Nicolas in his car seat with the fastidiousness of rookie parents. Finally, emerging from the garage, I had the vague sensation of having stolen a baby. I still did not discount the possibility there had been a mistake in our billing. And I hardly had been able to do anything by myself with him for the entirety of his life—did my task-masters really sign off on us leaving? Apparently yes, we were cleared to go. Ready or not. Sitting in the car, I was awash with post partum's mixed emotions: confidence, a touch of trepidation, but most important, a sublime happiness at the existence of my new family.

"Thank you for coming on such short notice." The lactation nurse smiled tersely and gingerly stepped into our apartment.

Whatever maternal skill I had possessed under the close supervision of the hospital nurses had apparently not accompanied me out of the hospital. Nor had Nicolas' ability to latch. Our first night home, in a wee morning hours moment of creative desperation, Josh and I took to feeding Nicolas expressed milk with an eye dropper, providing temporarily staying his cries. At breakfast the following morning, we stared at each other over giant cups of coffee, shell-shocked; Nicolas' howls still reverberated in our ears. Clearly in need of help, we placed an urgent call to a lactation specialist.

Cutting a formidable figure in our small apartment, the nurse promptly started her inquiry. "Where do you bathe the baby?"

I was mortified. I pointed to our kitchen sink, which at that moment was a vision of precariously stacked plates and bits of day-old food. Our shower had an oddly shaped tub basin that would have made bathing a baby difficult. Also, I knew generations of my ancestors had been bathed in a sink, survived, and went on to produce offspring who would do despicable things like also bathe their babies in sinks. Unfortunately, we had not yet cleaned up from Josh's surprise 30th birthday dinner the evening before. Our parents, who had flown in from the States, had helped me pull off the party, but we hadn't gotten around to whipping the kitchen back into a respectable state. Without them there wasn't much I could accomplish. Carrying Nicolas around all day made me as useful as a Tyrannosaurus rex, possessing only helpless, stubby arms.

Nurse Judgy Pants pursed her lips and turned to survey the rest of the apartment; the party streamers still hanging from the ceiling wilted under her gaze. Doubtlessly contemplating the necessity of calling Brazil's Child Protective Services, she next asked, "May I see the baby?"

I took her to the crib where Nicolas was sleeping and, after a brief examination, she gravely pronounced, "He is freezing cold." He was wearing a full-coverage pajama, but lacked additional layers. I nodded submissively and nervously went over to the bins where his clothes were stored. Nicolas had been born during a cold, rainy period in September, during which clothes never seemed to dry. We, like many in Brazil, did not have the luxury of a dryer. Most residences in the country, including ours, also lacked central air or heating.

Thus, the inside of our apartment was as cold and damp as the outside—reaching between 50 and 60 degrees in the winter months. Sure, a self-respecting Minnesotan like me could not declare the cool temperature as cold. But it certainly was unpleasant never to have an escape from the chill.

Compounding the problem, Nicolas often required several outfit changes a day due to diaper blowouts and I had purchased a limited quantity of the newborn size. The sage, experienced mothers of the internet had advised me to do so, and I did not appreciate how the "newborn" and "0-3 month" size actually differed; "A newborn *is* zero months old," I reasoned. Well, the 0-3 size dwarfed his small frame. And to keep him clothed at all, my mom had taken to washing clothes continually and then painstakingly drying them with a blow dryer. Looking into the bin, I prayed the current output of our protracted supply chain would satisfy the nurse's ominous demands.

To my great relief I found a suitable outfit, and I began to put it on the now awake Nicolas. To my amateur observation his limbs felt a normal temperature, and I saw no other indication that he was cold. Staring at me with furrowed intensity, Nurse Judgy Pants instructed, "Babies should always have one more layer than adults."

I would later come to understand her criticism as an echo of the golden rule of caring for children in Brazil: when in doubt, they are cold. I was surprised when the hospital nurses had brought Nicolas back from his first bath resembling a little Michelin Man, wearing nearly all the clothes I had packed for our entire stay. Even as the Brazilian summer arrived in force I was still subject to the scrutiny of the street grandma vigilantes, who would make helpful observations such as, "Excuse me, ma'am, are you aware your baby is not wearing socks?" When I later mentioned this extra layer rule to my Norwegian grandma, I had to laugh when she replied, "Oh really? I thought it was one *less* layer." Eleanor RoJeana lived her whole life in northern Minnesota's farm country. She loved to tell the story of how she and her twin sister survived their premature birth by being placed together in a shoebox with a hot water bottle, their medical care constituting visits from a country nurse.

In my current fragile state, however, I absorbed a pound of judgment with every ounce of advice. We finished the consultation uneventfully enough with Nurse Judgy Pants' suggestions for improved latching. Finally ushering her out, I rested my head against the closed door, only to notice the still-scattered confetti festively mocking me.

Looking down at Nicolas, who now seemed impossibly scrawny, yellowish, and most likely freezing cold, I tearfully asked my mom, "Do you think we should do it? The two terrible days?"

Several days had passed with little success nursing Nicolas. I had just seen another lactation nurse who recommended letting Nicolas nurse only if he latched on his own, estimating that within "two terrible days" our problem would be solved. Starting with the eye dropper and expanding to a nipple guard, nursing training wheels of sorts, I had relied on gimmicks to keep Nicolas fed. Still, his pediatrician was worried about his weight, and on top of that, she had diagnosed him with jaundice. The solution to his jaundice was simple enough: two sunbaths daily. Yet the weather conspired to hand me another maternal failure by sending only endless rain. Determined not to add to my lengthening new mother rap sheet, I was willing to take drastic measures to resolve Nicolas' latching problem. I did not want to fail motherhood before I even started! At the same time, I sure was not going to do anything unless my mom said so.

The challenges of motherhood had caught me completely

unprepared, bringing me to a state that I thought I had long outgrown: needing a mommy of my own, someone on whom I could completely depend. My own maternal skills and instincts MIA, I did not trust myself to make a correct decision. Nor could I rely on the sometimes-tyrannical lactation nurses. In a cloud of physical and emotional exhaustion, I also knew I could not see it through on my own. Josh, besides also being devoid of maternal instinct, had been understandably preoccupied trying to save his company. So it was my mom who huddled with me in the corner of my bedroom, helping me decide, stroking my hair, and catching my tears.

To my two terrible days query, my mom replied, "Yes, let's do it. I'll be here by your side."

"All right," I said nervously, "Let's start now."

Thus, we began a trial-and-error process in which I would contort my body every which way while my mom would maneuver Nicolas. Various nurses had offered conflicting advice, one advising "hunch forward in a position of reverence" another "keep your shoulders firmly back," leaving us completely confused, with perseverance as our only strategy. When we eventually stumbled upon success, I bit my lip to channel the accompanying pain, not daring to move lest we have to start the whole process again. And so it went, every three hours as required by the pediatrician. A force less strong than a mother's love would not have seen us persist through the night, endure the cold, or withstand sleep deprivation.

My grandpa, Eugene Kennedy, known for his Irish wit, was fond of saying one can survive any day provided it starts with a hot shower and ends with wine or ice cream. Unfortunately, we had no ability to take a hot shower when our shower broke, and neither Josh nor I had any bandwidth to chase down the landlord to fix it. Forced to make do with only half of the *pater familias*' advice for survival of tough times, I staggered on to the second "terrible day." Never before having experienced such anguish and fatigue, I was turned into a tormented zombie.

The next day I was again huddled in the corner of the bedroom, my near permanent post where I nursed and rocked Nicolas. My mom had left to give Josh and me some privacy to talk. Reading Josh's disconsolate body language, I braced myself for the update from his day. He was alternatively scrambling to find investors and meeting with bankruptcy lawyers to prepare for any contingency. Unlike that of the United States, Brazil's legal system did not allow for a true limited liability, meaning in the event of bankruptcy, creditors could seek redress from our (laughably nonexistent) personal assets. Owners of defunct companies unable to completely pay all their creditors have a "dirty name" and find it near impossible to complete basic functions in Brazilian life. This grim context in mind, I listened to his report.

"I need you to get Nicolas his passports as soon as possible. I'm not sure if at some point we will have to leave in a hurry." Nicolas, a dual citizen, would need passports from both Brazil and the United States to travel.

"What? Like flee under the cover of darkness?"

"Something like that. I'm still seeing what our options are with my lawyers."

Looking down, I tearfully surveyed the collection of English-language children's books that had arrived in a half-dozen suitcases of different relatives. I had coordinated this effort because I wanted to share my love of reading with my child, and I knew I could not expect to find certain classics of children's literature locally. What would be the fates of *Goodnight Moon* or *The Very Hungry Caterpillar* in the event of an abrupt, covert exodus?

"What an awful way to go. Like criminals. With all our hard work counting for nothing. Leaving behind the life we have built."

Josh sat silently. He did not need to respond. We both knew leaving now would mean arriving at my in-laws' house with a newborn, four suitcases, precarious balance sheet, and our broken dreams. We would have to start anew from the ignominious position of having brought a company to the ground.

"Okay" I sighed, my eyes red from exhaustion and too many tears. "I'll try to figure out the paperwork tomorrow."

The priest at *Santuário Nossa Senhora de Fátima* (Our Lady of Fatima Church) rapped on the tabernacle door, summoning the special protection of the parish's patron for our newborn son. We were not familiar with this baptismal tradition, but still raw from our recent struggles, we welcomed any and all protection and blessing upon our little family, which had suffered such a tumultuous start. I had tossed up more than one desperate prayer to the Blessed Mother since tearing past her statue in the maternity ward. Mother to mother, I knew she had been with me in my newborn vigils. I welcomed the opportunity to sit peacefully in her presence.

Emerging from the church into the bright sunlight, we walked back down the hill to enjoy a celebratory meal. As they had been doing all week, my in-laws, God bless their Texas hearts, served up plates of comfort, strength, and hospitality from our tiny city kitchen. My dad, the consummate statesman, washed dishes with the sleeves of his sport coat rolled up. And my mom continued to cheerlead my wobbly first mothering steps.

Enveloped in this loving support, Josh and I rested wearily, having survived the recent trials and not yet required to tackle those of tomorrow. Nicolas' next pediatric appointment would see him back on track for weight. The two days were indeed terrible, but the second lactation nurse was correct. And Josh had scraped together a painful deal with his existing investors that allowed us to live to fight another quarter.

10

TURBULENCE

As I entered the terminal, adrenaline and terror pumped through my veins in equal measure. I was about to embark on an important rite of passage for an expat mom (indeed, any mom), my first solo flight with a tot. I was on hyper alert for any indication that my tiny traveling companion was considering letting loose with one of his trademark meltdowns.

Months earlier, I had put a flight tracker on a trip back to Minnesota for Thanksgiving. While blissfully lodged at the maternity ward I received an email informing me the price of my flight had dropped by $600. Scrambling to find the hospital wi-fi code, I booked the cheapest flight home I had ever purchased for Nicolas and me; Josh, unfortunately, was unable to take off for both Thanksgiving and Christmas. The moment's thought I had given to the challenges inherent in flying solo with a baby before clicking "purchase" had haunted me in high-definition detail as the trip approached.

The possibility of a screaming baby for the entirety of the 10-hour international leg, as contemplated by my paranoia, seemed eminently possible considering recent experience. Nicolas continued to be a fussy baby even after the nursing difficulties. One memorable Sunday, he cried literally the whole day despite our best efforts to soothe him. Assuming that our status as first-time parents was partially to blame, Josh and I amused ourselves (in a partially successful effort to stay sane) by narrating his cries: “New parents! I told the hospital I wanted new parents! I put my request in weeks ago! Waaah!”

A spate of relatives had visited, but when the last of them left, I gathered Nicolas in my arms and sobbed, “It’s just you and me, kid. Let’s figure this out together.” My confidence, though, was in tatters from my rough start. Shame demanded I hide my fussy baby and maternal failings in the privacy of my own home. When I was able to beat back my fears and brave the world outdoors, the same grandmotherly figures who previously hailed me as a wonderful, life-giving force now only seemed to offer couched criticism in the guise of innocuous questions. In possession of a crying baby in public, I was a sitting duck for astute suggestions like, “Is he hungry?” Accepting their inquiry with a weak smile, I would locate the nearest escape route while hotly fuming, “Ah yes, *hungry*. Why hadn’t I thought of that?” I was open to receiving advice from trusted sources—namely my mom and our pediatrician. But this unsolicited advice smacked of the arrogance of the casual observer. “In a matter of seconds, with a brief glance, I have performed a comprehensive analysis of your life’s core struggle and, in my infinite wisdom, have divined an obvious solution that has thus far escaped you and your feeble efforts at a resolution.” Their words were a sudden spotlight, a flashing red beeping warning signal, announcing, “Alert! Alert! We have detected the presence of a bad mom. All capable hands please report to the scene. Provide advice—stat!” Even when Nicolas was content, these ubiquitous, meddling grandmas would still seek and find areas for improvement: a strap that looked too tight or the possible choking risks of a teething toy. And, of course, there was always their golden go-to, he might be cold. With all that echoing inside my head, now I would expose myself to 20-odd hours of travel and scrutiny with my notoriously challenging baby, and I was terrified. But my commitment to family, a force stronger than my fear, propelled me onward.

Feigning confidence and calm, I progressed through the familiar hurdles of international travel, eventually making it to our seat. The hour was long past his bedtime, so I began the extreme bouncing sequence, resembling a series of squats, that best worked to put Nicolas to sleep. (In another moment of desperation in the wee hours, Josh and I had discovered that Nicolas was most comforted by rocking, bouncing, and swinging that bordered on turbulence.) It worked. He slept! I was dumbfounded; in the million nightmare scenarios I imagined pre-flight, I never contemplated the possibility that he might actually sleep. Having scored the seat that allowed for a bassinet add-on, I tucked him into his sky-high berth. I fell into an uneasy sleep until the sound of whimpering sprung me into action again.

Most days since Nicolas was born, I fell into bed at day's end, weary but content, having had the privilege of expending every bit of my energy contributing to the flourishing of a life. Slowly, slowly I had learned how to take care of my baby—even though my confidence had yet to catch up. I knew which cry meant hungry, which cry meant tired, and how to soothe him with extreme aerobics. Just as I had promised him in the quiet of our apartment, we figured it out together. Nicolas rewarded my efforts the first time he smiled at me with recognition, as if to say, "You are my mommy and I love you for it." It was just a little smile, but it evoked a tidal wave of euphoria. I was completely enamored with my baby, and I willingly devoted myself to him. My shoulders used to ache from hours hunched over a computer, preparing a schedule or memo for some soon-forgotten, esoteric use. Now I ached from disjointed sleep and the physical labor of caring for my son. In this heady emotion of new love,

I was happy to pretend I had no needs of my own so I might more fully commit myself to him.

Having begun to master the mechanics of craft, I embraced study as I developed my own particular style of motherhood. I had recently set up an audio book account and found that I had ample time to listen in the hours I spent rocking a baby. I gravitated toward the biographies of great mothers, such as Rose Kennedy and Queen Victoria, for inspiration in charting my new role. True to my guiding credo, I again wanted to apply my talents to their highest and best use, and I expected my efforts to yield results. This time I was sure I would not fail.

I saw an intimate example of what was possible in my own grandma, the disciplined German matriarch of the spirited clan who gifted my youth with a sense of purpose and camaraderie. Alvina Dorothy fervently believed in serving God and country—and the power of education to change lives. Her determination motivated every one of her seven children to become first-generation college graduates. Thanks to her thrifty economy, my dad and all his siblings received $500 toward each year of their four-year degrees and an additional $500 toward a study abroad program. It was impossible for her to consider a liberal arts education without an international experience, though she had never left the United States. One of her 27 grandchildren, I grew up with a band of merry cousins that, for all our fun-loving ways, was committed to carrying her values into the future. This was the family I was braving precarious international "baby and me" travel to visit. If my grandma could survive the trials inherent in raising seven children, I could certainly survive an airplane ride with only one.

Nicolas and I landed in Chicago the next morning to another sprint through the usual travel hurdles, plus a diaper change. I suddenly realized these were my son's first moments on U.S. soil, and I looked for an auspicious place to take his photo. Finding nothing particularly suitable, I settled on the best available option: the golden arches of a McDonald's adorned with a slew of American flags.

I survived the domestic leg with a combination of a "who cares, I'm almost there" abandon and the comfort of being surrounded by the familiar archetypes of my youth; quintessential Minnesotan grandmotherly figures readily bestowed heaping compliments on both my baby and my gallant efforts to transport him to the land of my birth.

Some 24 hours after leaving our apartment in São Paulo, I triumphantly gave the stroller one last push through the automated doors that separate arriving passengers from waiting loved ones and collapsed into the jubilant embraces of my mom, sister, brother, and sister-in-law. Picking up where the airplane grandmas had left off, my family dutifully but genuinely *oohed* and *aahed* over the newest member of the clan and the first of its next generation.

11

CONTINUING EDUCATION

I plopped down on the sheet-draped couch and carefully positioned my paint-stained clothes to allow Nicolas to nurse, free of toxins.

As Nicolas was soon mobile, we had recently moved to a kid-friendly apartment. The neighborhood had much to recommend it, including one of São Paulo's few decent parks, a bakery that sold the perfect crunchy-outside, soft-inside baguette, a beautiful parish church, and a first-rate urgent care facility. The apartment itself was perfectly functional, but as highly practical things often are, decidedly *not* elegant or even close to cool. Duct tape held my appliances together in more spots than one. A kitschy fruit-themed tile spanned the kitchen walls. But the *piéce de résistance* was the living room statement piece: a jumbo, frayed, sagging couch in a commanding shade of fire engine red. Despite these flaws, I had an affinity toward the apartment from the first time I toured it, knowing its price and location made it the home my family needed.

After a joyous visit to Minnesota where Nicolas and I were embraced and enveloped by family and friends, my mom had flown back with us to take care of Nicolas while I poured my heart and muscle into transforming the apartment space into a suitable nest. My current task, giving new life to dingy walls with a fresh coat of paint, was reminiscent of the many times I served as a conscript in my Grandma Alvina's army of painters, her German frugality not countenancing the expense of a professional when she could tap into the human resources of her clan. The matching towels hanging in the bathrooms were another triumph. The towels that Josh and I individually acquired upon our arrival in Brazil had expanded to a collection of misfit blues every time a visitor required another acquisition. Unable to face my impending 30th birthday with a college dormitory-esque towel collection, I earmarked some gift money for a matching set.

While preparing each room for habitation, I happily dreamed about the possibilities for each space. Looking down at Nicolas, I imagined the many firsts he would have in this apartment—with my crisp, white "Snowbound" paint as a backdrop. I even felt a preemptive nostalgia for the day that we would eventually leave this home.

When Nicolas finished nursing, I held him up to gaze at a face that was changing daily only to catch him at the onset of a wail, bringing my visions of maternal golden years crashing back to reality. I was perplexed. He was far less prone to fussiness than he had been as a newborn. My mom peeked in and suggested, "Maybe he is still hungry?" I sighed, knowing she was probably right. I had been reluctant to admit that Nicolas had been nursing a lot recently. Now forced to face the distressing realization that I was responsible for preparing meals for another human being, a few tears of my own leaked out. I could barely keep myself fed! How was I to feed another?

Motherhood had elevated my long-standing battle with my ultimate nemesis—staving off hunger. Josh joked that I personified Maslow's hierarchy of needs, completely losing my ability to function when hungry. One long Saturday at the office during the Petrobras project, I unexpectedly found myself crying when it became clear that we would not be able to finish our work in time and go home for dinner. I was genuinely surprised by these tears, having a firm resolve never to cry at the office. I had a few embarrassing outbursts during my New York boot camp, but these tears were completely beyond my ability to control; it was as if I were crying "feed me!" for the baby.

My appetite only increased as my time to prepare food decreased. While I found many tasks difficult with a baby shadow, I particularly struggled with cooking; my skills were rudimentary at best. I had long since detached myself from requiring a tasty, or even hot meal, instead evaluating food solely on its ability to resolve my hunger. My only firm requirement was that my coffee be hot, finding it was key to activating my secret mom powers after yet another sleep-deprived day.

I had read an article that said many women unexpectedly find themselves stay-at-home moms after being caught off-guard by the time and effort it takes to raise children.[4] I, too, had been unpleasantly surprised by the amount of additional work that followed the birth of my first child. It seemed I had to exert tremendous effort just to maintain a veneer of respectability and responsibility on the whole chaotic operation.

As my maternity leave came to a close, I was fortunate to find a job that allowed me to continue working and alleviated my household burden. My alma mater opened an office in São Paulo shortly after Nicolas was born and I networked my way into a job that, as I had humbly hoped, allowed me to be a hands-on mom while helping to meet our bills. Starting my working mom life, I entrusted Nicolas to our long-time cleaning lady turned nanny. Household help was widely affordable in Brazil. Our middle-class apartment included a space we used as a storage closet, that, 20 years earlier, had been used as a bedroom for a live-in maid. Our housekeeper extraordinaire,

Helena, was a gem of a woman and a blessing to our family. Growing up in northeastern Brazil, she was the little mother to a half-dozen younger siblings. This training earned her the nickname *Flash* and enabled her to take charge of our one baby and much of our apartment's household work as if they were no challenge at all.

Even with help at a level my American peers could only imagine, I still found myself running from Nicolas' first squawk to collapsing into bed at day's end. It was clear my drastic shift from the life of a professional to that of a homemaker left me in significant need of on-the-job training, cooking being the area most in need of remedial education.

My mom cheerily interrupted my tearful musings, "Let's try him on solid food. Come on into the kitchen. I'll show you." I watched her smash up a banana and feed it to an enthusiastic Nicolas.

Sure, smashing up a banana was easy enough, but he would soon require more robust fare and my kitchen's output—sandwiches, the occasional soup or chicken breast, and yet more sandwiches—was barely sustaining me. I could no longer skirt the homemaker expertise I had never deemed relevant to learn, having prioritized achievement over traditional female roles. Now I had no choice. I had to acquire new skills.

Emboldened by a French parenting book I had recently finished, I implemented the "High Chair Confinement Program" as my survival tactic of choice. French parenting was all the rage around the time Nicolas was born. I was not one to follow a trend, but the author was a fellow expat mom, and I felt a kinship in her tales of cultural mishaps. She stressed the importance of considering the welfare of the entire family (mommy included) when making decisions and encouraged parents to look for opportunities to teach their children patience. So, I secured Nicolas safely in his high chair, provided him with a diverting rotation of toys, books, and even kitchen utensils, and then focused on deciphering a recipe and then making it.

In time, I built a repertoire of meals that I could reliably prepare while exhausted, already hungry, or with Nicolas losing his mind. I fell back on techniques employed by mothers who came before me: employing the same 10 or so recipes in rotation, wielding the power of the freezer so one dish could yield multiple meals, and making heavy use of the crockpot—that magical kitchen appliance that requires no supervision and has heavy-duty protein ready just in time for dinner.

Despite this automation, I never became a natural cook and the kitchen remained a battle ground. Ancillary to the cooking front was the staying on top of the dishes sans dishwasher, another appliance not common in Brazil. My commitment to winning this battle of the suds bordered on obsessive. I dared not face the unknowns of the next round of combat with anything less than optimal starting conditions.

12

SPECIAL WORLD

I kept a step behind Nicolas as he explored our neighborhood park. Now a bona fide toddler, Nicolas had an infectious zest for life and its possibilities. He found endless delight in the experiences provided by our nearly daily park excursions. He reveled in the sensation of sand falling through his fingers, the spectacle of poultry on parade, and the rumble of the maintenance tractor. But by far his favorite playthings were nature's simple materials: rocks, sticks, and leaves.

Today Nicolas settled on a particular pile of rocks. I sat on a nearby tree stump, deeply content observing him engrossed in play. During such idle moments of motherhood, my unattended thoughts were liable to float a pesky question: "Why am I here instead of a nanny?" I had always aspired to use my talents to their highest and best use. But, I wondered, "Was it really my highest and best use to watch my kid play?" Reading about child development left the distinct impression that all our interactions were rife with implications for Nicolas' future IQ and happiness. Yet it seemed any competent adult could have provided my laissez-faire supervision from the tree stump.

Like many of my peers, I was raised with the optimistic call to have it all: a flourishing career *and* family. Girl power, Destiny's Child's "Independent Women," and Sheryl Sandberg's *Lean In* were anthems of my generation. At the same time, our mothers and grandmothers' way of life continued to hold merit; girls were raised to understand family life required significant time and dedication. Achieving adulthood, I experienced the conflicting pressure to work as if I did not have a personal life and devote myself to my child as if I had no other commitments, particularly work. How was this supposed to add up? As a child I had never thought to question its feasibility. But now, immersed in its ramifications, I could neither imagine nor understand how a mere mortal could simultaneously succeed at both.

A cool breeze hit my face, and I smiled in appreciation of my park sanctuary. Here, beneath a canopy of palm trees, these nagging doubts did not hold as much sway over me. My heart told me I was where I needed to be, even though my head could not explain why. I had grown in maternal confidence and knew something good and beautiful was unfolding before me. I also had the benefit of an important layer of protection from culture and its messy pressures: my geography. Long the awkward foreigner, I felt little pressure to conform to the standards represented by my environment, whether it be eating a sandwich with a fork and knife or pretending I knew anything about *futebol.* Yes, I made a good faith effort to respect my host country's culture and no, I did not always like being the odd one out. But whether I liked it or not, expat life had taught me to be more comfortable with breaking from the crowd. And the American moms, critics, and scolds who could more effectively hold me to account were sparse on the ground. Thus, from my serene perch in a Brazilian jungle oasis, I had an invaluable blank page on which to write my way.

Endowed with this unusual freedom, I chose simple, outdoor play as a key tenet of the special world I was striving to create. I called it "toodle time." During toodle time I let Nicolas decide the course of play, was responsive to him, but did not interrupt him when he was focused. True to my analytical, ambitious nature, I endorsed "play" only after great deliberation. Since Nicolas was born I had listened to a half dozen more audiobooks on topics ranging from Montessori principles to child brain development to emotional intelligence. And in the many long, somewhat solitary days that had passed since becoming a mother, I had mulled over what I had absorbed from these books, considering how they might affect the object of my perpetual observation. I was aware of the practice of intensive parenting, a child development arms race instigated by a competitive global economy. Daily alphabet and number drills would seem like the natural choice for an over-achiever such as myself. Yet I demurred. Reading of the life and work of Dr. Maria Montessori, the pioneering Italian physician and Catholic whose system of education bears her name, inclined me toward prioritizing a child's natural interests and activities over formal teaching methods. And the mommy blog advice—"the harder your brain is working, the less their brain is working"—best resonated with what my own experience had taught me: a lasting love of learning comes from within.

Nicolas, having created a rock formation particularly to his liking, manifested his excitement with his trademark move of simultaneously slapping his knees while hopping. I marveled at his effortless, impromptu, energetic joy—and I laughed. His joy was my joy.

Going outside was always our first entertainment choice. My recent experiences in Vitamin D and green space deprivation had left me with a deep appreciation of the park's expansive, lush terrain. As for Nicolas, I had early learned that fresh air was one of the best remedies for his fussy moods, either allowing him to submit to sleep or forget his baby woes in the distraction of a big, new world unfolding around him. Emboldened by my discovery, I would purposely load a screaming Nicolas in the baby carrier, praying that I would not be trapped in the elevator with any judgy grandmas in our descent to freedom.

Even as Nicolas outgrew his newborn fussiness, we continued to go outside as soon as my morning housework hustle allowed to keep us both from feeling stir-crazy. While Nicolas needed an outlet for his interminable energy, I, too, required leaving my nest daily with the dignity conferred by a spit-up free shirt and a dab of lipstick. In coming to value this outdoor time we embraced the Norwegian adage: "There is no bad weather, only bad clothes." While from my tropical latitude I could hardly boast of climate courage on par with authentic Norwegians, we bravely ventured out in conditions considered unthinkable by local standards: rain and temperatures below 70 Fahrenheit. When predictably accosted by the officious street grandmas, my new confidence allowed me to coyly respond, "Oh, no, we're not cold. We're *North* American."

The neighborhood park, *Parque da Água Branca*, had come serendipitously into our life and held a beloved place in our little world. I had first visited our park on a blind play date and was immediately gripped by the notion that I simply must have access to this space. Before this playdate I understood São Paulo to have precious few parks, and none that we could feasibly live by. While I had worked in our park's vicinity for several years, its graffiti-stained, faded yellow walls had shielded it as skillfully from me as it did from the grime and hubbub of the city. Thus, each new area we toured ignited an explorer's thrill, happening upon playgrounds, reading cabins, a senior citizen center, a riding arena, fish ponds, free range chickens, ducks, peacocks, cats, and even monkeys—this was the tropics after all! But best of all was the ability to see greenery in every direction. My attention was decidedly distracted from the usual topic of play date conversation, namely exchanging ideas on how we can get our little dears to sleep more. This discovery was fortuitously timed; we began our search for a new apartment soon after this play date and proximity to this park was my principal consideration.

Nicolas toodled over to my stump, offering me a choice rock with his magnetic smile. I accepted his gift as if accepting a precious jewel, partaking in his wonder.

More accustomed to being a faceless resident of my most recent megacity, I was pleasantly surprised when our daily excursions established Nicolas and me as recognized individuals, regulars almost. Not long after we moved in, the attendant at the neighborhood bakery began to address me as *mãe* (mother) whether I was with Nicolas or not. In time, I could run into people I knew from one place at another place, such as the ladies who admired Nicolas at church on Sunday and then delighted in having another chance to coo over him at Tuesday's farmers market.

At the park, the public square of our special world, we had privileged access to the coffee, crackers, and gab on offer by the "Millennial Club." Our senior friends had given themselves the moniker figuring their combined ages totaled at least a thousand. Over time this friendship revealed a delightful cast of characters. Zulema was the Argentine *grande dame* who served up both coffee and conversation. Mauricio, the husband who had whisked her away from her beloved homeland, was a retired pediatrician who contented himself relating the same banal advice to me day after day; "I saw Nicolas. I saw Nicolas eat a cracker off the ground. Tell him he cannot do that." (Notably absent was his prescription for categorically making a toddler do anything.) Ricardo was a kind-hearted gentleman who arrived early to reserve the group's preferred table, entertaining himself in the interval by enticing tropical birds to the table with cracker crumbs. Wanda was a Polish emigrant whose wise, mirthful spirit made her esteemed. Marie Stella was the group's centenarian who proudly attributed her longevity to frequenting the park, with its "best air in São Paulo," since she was nine. And Pinheiro was the club jester, entertaining Nicolas with his Donald Duck impression and the group with his guitar.

I cherished the recognition I received from my neighborhood friends for the same reason I had cherished The Crazy Cat Man's heroic efforts on my behalf—as proof that I was part of the community. Yes, I was still lonely; pleasantries, current events, and the occasional pearl of wisdom were the contours of these relationships. At the same time, I appreciated having these many someones to greet me, notice if I were absent, watch the baby when the toddler made a run for it, and collect a toy I had forgotten. Culture, language, age, and myriad other factors may have prevented them from fixing my loneliness, but did not prevent us from caring about one another.

Concluding our morning, Nicolas and I headed back up the long, sloping sidewalk that led home with pleasant remembrances of a good day's adventure.

13

RETREAT

Recently, Josh and I had been overjoyed to learn I was pregnant again. It had always been our intention to have a proper brood and we thought it best to have them closer in age—better for sibling camaraderie and to compress the years of our life spent changing diapers.

I had just put Nicolas down for a nap, and I was eager to log into my computer to check the results of my latest prenatal bloodwork. While I had been successful incorporating Nicolas into many chores thanks to my Highchair Confinement Program and other initiatives, attempting any task on the computer with him hovering had repeatedly proved futile, a frustrating, never-ending game of "Mommy, what does this button do?" Thankfully, Nicolas had evolved from taking a series of fitful power naps to one long, glorious afternoon nap. Nestled on our red couch, I scrolled past incomprehensible medical jargon in search of the only thing I understood or cared about: Zika.

Around the time of Nicolas' birth, an outbreak of Zika fever in Brazil garnered international attention as evidence grew that it was the cause of another epidemic: babies being born with microcephaly, or a smaller than normal brain and head. Previously, Zika was considered a mild infection and not known to have other adverse effects. When babies born afflicted by microcephaly showed up in other parts of South America, North America, and on several islands in the Pacific and Southeast Asia, the World Health Organization declared Zika a "Public Health Emergency of International Concern."[5] A novel disease, there were many unknowns and no effective treatments, all of which were of enormous concern to parents who were expecting.

This grim tidal wave of a scary, unknown, evolving threat made the Aedes aegypti mosquito, responsible for transmitting the infection, my Public Enemy Number 1. The nearly 2,000 miles between our São Paulo home and ground zero of the Brazilian outbreak, in the country's northeast, gave me little comfort. Per my obstetrician's recommendation I had special window screens installed in our apartment and daily applied repellent so potent it could double as a nail polish remover, a fact I learned when it wrecked my fresh manicure.

Haunted by the horrific possibilities, I lay awake at night staring at the screens allegedly capable of protecting me from what I would walk out into the morning anyway. I might have contemplated sequestration had I not already had a child, but as it was, our collective sanity and the need for diapers and groceries demanded our daily excursions. Despite radiating an invisible wave of bug spray every time I stepped out, I still had the occasional bite and agonized over each one.

Scrolling scrolling....Zika...result: undetermined.

Jarred, I looked for clarity in the details. The supporting schedules ruthlessly communicated a terrible truth: my blood could not definitively be declared Zika-free.

As if I had been punched in the gut, I reflexively hunched over in gasping sobs. My mind reeled in a tortured haze, recalling all the pictures of small-headed babies and their bleak diagnoses I had seen in headline news.

I called my obstetrician who vainly tried to assure me that "undetermined" was not "determined," the tests were designed to be sensitive, and that I should avoid drawing conclusions until I could retake the test in a week's time. Hysteria giving no credence to a possible bright side, I hung up the phone and continued sob-gasping.

Besides a nightmare, this sterile medical report decisively shattered the shield I had been pretending existed around my special world. In my new routine I had largely disengaged from the world beyond my strolling radius. My isolation was in part a natural byproduct of my circumstances, motherhood and expat life, and part an effort to block out that which I found unpleasant.

When I became a mother, I renewed my efforts to find a circle of friends, focusing on other new moms. For a time, I enjoyed a pleasant lineup of play dates until the usual churn of expat life saw my acquaintances move on. Moreover, Nicolas had recently outgrown his infant car seat that had allowed us to zip around the city in a taxi; I now had to drive when traveling beyond the limits of our special world. Having relied on public transportation most of my adult life, my driving experience was largely limited to rural Minnesota roads, which left me ill-equipped for São Paulo's notoriously difficult traffic. Add one precious passenger with a volatile temperament and my fear of driving bordered on phobia.

Loneliness, however, trumped that potent fear, and one day I braved traveling to a playdate in the throes of my new pregnancy's nausea, only to get hopelessly lost and have an irate Nicolas throw up everywhere. I had long lamented the amount of effort required to establish a modicum of friendship and deliberated whether it was even worth it. That afternoon—scrubbing partially digested breakfast from a car seat's myriad crannies, fighting the urge to throw up myself, never having made it to the playdate—my answer was a definitive "No."

And what about establishing other adult relationships? Participating in social events of the normal, non-playdate variety only served as an unwelcome reminder of my abdication of the game I once played. The São Paulo startup crowd had a social intensity on par with that of New York. With their companies (and chance at a proper livelihood) nearly always facing existential pressures in the form of flirtations with bankruptcy, Josh and his fellow entrepreneurs maintained "pitch mode," a near-permanent state of peppiness and strength designed to squelch doubt. It was most effectively dispelled with quick wit and ready answers. While I had previously enjoyed the thrill of such high-pressure repartee, I now found myself lacking fluency regardless of the conversation's language. Sure, I had a job I could talk up. But I did not want to try. I was jaded by earlier experiences with self-aggrandizing talk. Additionally, I knew my true passion, motherhood, held negative social value. Even I struggled to appreciate stories about other people's kids. Acutely aware that I was a social zero, I naturally gravitated toward seclusion over a dressing down of my confidence.

Not that I had many invitations to decline; throughout our life abroad Josh and I found our social schedule puzzlingly sparse. We had tried recreating New York's dinner parties only to find guests in short supply, preparation significantly more complicated with a baby, and our tacky apartment furnishings woefully inadequate for "pitch mode." Output again not compensating for effort, we eventually gave up. Even my previously robust interest in current events had similarly evaporated; having given up on saving the world, I struggled to find affairs of states relevant. And as steward of a child's innocence, I found it harder to absorb news of the tragic, heinous, or otherwise disheartening.

I was aware of my gradual retreat and I wondered if fulfillment was somehow tucked away somewhere inside my special world. There was certainly much about it that brought me satisfaction. I loved witnessing Nicolas flourish in a world I had created. On days I was not at the office, I had been able to shape our routine to my liking, spending the better part of the morning playing in a jungle oasis and the afternoon resting and reading. Nevertheless, I could not shake the feelings of discontent and loneliness that frustrated my idyllic isolation. The day's news of a possible Zika diagnosis only served to obliterate defenses long ago compromised.

Zika Zika ZIKA. I knew I could expect no relief from this piercing, awful worry.

Then again, it was just another unforeseen consequence of our decision to risk jungle life. Little of the canvas I had imagined wandering neighborhoods our first year in Brazil had materialized. The threadbare, obnoxious red couch on which I sat was an ever-present reminder of the stresses, dismal family finances, and social isolation we had endured throughout our life in Brazil. But this worry, one that threatened the health of my unborn child, stung far worse than all the rest. It carried the potential for the worst guilt a mother can bear: the failure to protect her child from harm.

Nap time having come to a close, I forced my look and bearing to be calm and controlled for Nicolas. Scary, possible prognosis of an evolving tropical disease certainly had no place in our special world. With a game face displaying excessive cheer, I resolutely enacted the song and dance routine that Nicolas daily required to overcome his post-nap grumpiness. "Hi! How are you!?! How about a snack and then we go to the playground? No? That sounds terrible? Okay. How about a snuggle?"

A week later the follow-up test definitively declared my blood Zika free. My doctor recommended we avoid testing for Zika for the remainder of my pregnancy, a suggestion to which I readily acquiesced. Why not hide from reality one more time? I could not hold both the reality that Zika was a real and present risk and my excitement at my growing family. Denial was the only way I knew how to protect my happiness from my fear. Failing strategy though it was, I had no other.

14

BABY BLUES REDUX

I stood outside our apartment building, savoring the day's warm sun and my pleasant anticipation of the weeks to come. My mother-in-law was soon to arrive from the airport, commencing what I hoped would be a relaxing wait during the final approach to my due date, about a month away.

In my first pregnancy I had felt social pressure from the street grandmas to avoid all exertion. "Am I just supposed to stay in bed and knit?!" I would complain to Josh. Now it seemed the neighborhood busybodies understood, as I did, that idleness was not an option; I already had a child who required care. Late into my third trimester, I had persevered through the combined physical strains of urban motherhood and pregnancy. Our car-less lifestyle meant I was a human minivan. Preparing to scale the hill home from the park, hauling one babe in utero and another in stroller, I would exhort myself, "If you did it yesterday you can do it today!" Neighborhood doormen and I had found mutual entertainment in my weekly grocery store run. They were amused by the sight of my ever-protruding belly as a counterweight to the loaded cart I dragged behind me. I was in turn was entertained by their bemused expressions and thoughts I felt I could read: "She's back *again*?!"

Now I could finally admit how challenging the last few weeks had been and how relieved I was to have help on the way. Ahead, I saw a stint of Texas-sized spoiling from my mother-in-law, concluding with a joyous coming together of family members to welcome our newest member. Already I buzzed with the unusual sensation of having benefited from an uninterrupted night's sleep; Josh and Nicolas had left for the States the day before to attend my brother's wedding. The trip presented new challenges for both of us. It was Josh's first time traveling solo with a tot and my first separation from said tot measured not in hours, but days.

Blinking into the bright sun, I saw the doorman waving to me and I speed waddled to our apartment's entrance, smiling with the happy reunion now imminent. Encountering not my mother-in-law but a messenger, my excitement turned to confusion. Receiving and then reading the messenger's letter, my bright outlook vaporized. I had been served legal papers, sued by the very hospital where I was planning on delivering a baby in the coming weeks. And as I knew all too well from my previous third trimester saga, the hospital's facilities represented my only chance to get a normal birth covered by our insurance plan.

The suit, while horribly inopportune, was not a complete surprise. Shortly after the birth of Nicolas we received an additional bill, the legitimacy of which we disputed. The hospital billing department had politely rejected our rationale and we, in turn, just as politely ignored their subsequent communications. I had naturally worried this approach might create problems for us the next time I was pregnant, but Josh assured me that we could quickly resolve them when necessary. Without extra resources to pay the bill anyway, I deferred to his judgment. And the nearly two years that had passed had lulled me with the false assurance that the hospital had dropped the issue.

Unceremoniously returned once again to that all too familiar state of hyper-stress, my brain made its customary leap to worst-case scenarios, which I began analyzing. I saw on one hand a ghastly public hospital birth and on the other, a private hospital scenario we certainly could not afford. The disputed bill, far less than the latter scenario, determined the clear course of action: reach a settlement ASAP.

A few days later, I stood outside our apartment building, joined by my mother-in-law, awaiting the return of Nicolas and Josh from their trip to the States. I was excited to scoop Nicolas up in my arms. Now that Josh was back, I hoped we would resolve this lawsuit quickly so I might get the stress-free end of pregnancy I desperately wanted, perhaps even deserved.

Nestled in my usual spot in the corner of the red couch, Josh sitting on the other end, I tried to assess my true feelings on our situation. The business that supported our family once again teetered on the precipice of bankruptcy, an eventuality that would involve laying off 120 employees and defaulting on millions in debt. Our only exit strategy remained fleeing to the safe harbor of my in-laws' house to reckon with the rubble of our life choices.

While we had painstakingly emerged from the red hole of our first-year free fall, our income never allowed for savings. Plagued by an American Protestant ethic (even though it was embedded in a Catholic) that equated financial failure with moral frivolity, our financial situation was an inextricable source of guilt. Recently, even our ability to meet our bills was suspect; Josh occasionally forwent his salary, the company's solvency requiring drastic measures. I approached our monthly family bill payments with foreboding.

Having lived this bankruptcy saga countless times before, its drama had seemingly lost its power, and I felt numb to the catastrophic possibility. Yet I wondered if I would be so aloof if I were actually forced to face the ruinous upheaval that often-feared catastrophe would bring to my growing family. Perhaps my principal stress, that of the still unresolved lawsuit, had clouded my perception. How could I worry about something as comparatively petty as commerce and financial security when my brain was reverberating with shrill hysterics of a far more primordial concern?

Indeed, the lawsuit was not resolved yet. While doing so was merely an administrative issue, Josh had not yet found the time to attend to it. When beseeched by his heavily pregnant wife, he would promise to see to it the next day. Yet, the next day always came with the same consuming problems: desperately trying to scrape together a fundraising round and deciding which vendors to pay and which not to pay—all while trying not to lose the company's hard-earned momentum. How could he worry about something as comparatively petty as a procedural matter when the survival of his company and the result of years of excruciating effort hung in the balance?

Swamped by his own problems, Josh lamely suggested that the hospital likely could not turn me away if I were in need of emergency services. In a state anything but zonked, he would have never even considered such a harebrained idea with his notoriously risk-averse wife. Imagine calling the insurance company to vet that hypothesis: "Suppose I am a debtor and defendant in a lawsuit to a hospital in your network, but I nevertheless arrived at this facility in active labor. Would you kick me out?" Hapless though his efforts were, I knew taking the matter over myself was futile. Josh was the family negotiator and I knew myself to be forever and always a nice Minnesotan.

Clearing all these messy thoughts with a deep sigh, I confessed, "I don't know how I'll feel if the company goes bankrupt and we have to go back home, but I do know I am spent. I don't have any energy left to give to this. We've been through it so many times."

He sighed. "You're probably right."

I tried to discern my husband's hidden thoughts, wondering how he would actually feel if handed a default on his dreams. All involved knew of the enormous effort he had made toward the company's success. Yet only I was privy to the brutal stress he felt and its effects: fitful nights, chronic pains otherwise unexplainable, and days spent wanting to throw up. I also knew the extent of his aspirations, the life he hoped to build for himself and our family, all perilously awaiting an investor's decision.

I slowly lowered my nine-month belly weight to the edge of the park sandbox. Finally managing to sit, I felt the now-familiar sensation of tiny feet trying to kick out new space in the vicinity of my ribs, displeased with the compressed real estate my current position allowed. While the sandbox ledge was hardly comfortable, it nevertheless was the place to be during my final days of pregnancy. Compensating for the discomfort was the opportunity to be immobile; the sand was always a magnet for Nicolas' attention. It also gave me an opportunity to apprise my mother-in-law of our latest in family drama. Unsurprisingly, the time that had passed since her arrival had been unusually tense.

I started on an upbeat note, addressing the issue that had been consuming. "What a relief about the settlement."

Josh had finally reached an agreement with the hospital, decreasing the household's collective stress and avoiding domestic combustion.

My own debilitating worry behind me, I curbed my frazzled emotions and projected the calm our home required. Josh, however, was still waiting for news from his potential investors. He had become a rattled shell: the even-keeled, loving man we knew and loved had been abducted by fearful anticipation.

"Yes, what a big relief," my mother-in-law replied, her characteristic cheerful demeanor never betraying the heartache I knew our extended foreign sojourn caused.

She would have far preferred to play with her grandson in a sandbox slightly closer than 5,000 miles away. My family, too, balanced being supportive of our dreams and preferring us closer. Our geography, for example, made it impossible for me, at this point in my pregnancy, to attend my own brother's wedding. We all keenly felt the difficulty in being there for each other in moments, both the mundane and the magnificent.

I gaily concluded, "Nothing to do now but wait!"

15

FLASH

Josh, we really should be getting to the hospital."

Two days past my due date, I had been having contractions periodically since dinner. The pain had been manageable, and I had carried on with our evening routine while making final preparations for the hospital. Earlier, Josh had stumbled upon me teary-eyed in our bedroom. When he asked what was wrong, I lamented, "When I get back everything will be different!" Having just tucked Nicolas in, our last bedtime just us two, bittersweet nostalgia effortlessly clobbered my fragile hormonal state.

Minutes later, the contractions suddenly intensified, and I was eager to trade sentimentality for medical attention. Josh was seated at the dining room table furiously typing. He mumbled, "Uh huh… can I just finish this email?" His mom peeked in from the kitchen to shoot him a look, doubling down on the one I was already giving him. He reluctantly closed his laptop. The calm bestowed by my second-time authority had apparently lulled my husband into the false security of a soon-to-be second-time parent. While last time I had put on a show of world-class flopping, the only pronounced display of emotion he had witnessed thus far was my clichéd mom tears and pronouncements that "my baby is growing up so fast!" From the high ground of having gotten my way on the decision to go to the hospital, I graciously forgave his lack of urgency.

We hugged my mother and father-in-law, on duty to shepherd Nicolas through the advent of his life as a big brother, and departed. A feeling of *déjà-vu* marked the journey; hadn't I already survived this dark of night, red light-prone, pothole-plagued, contraction-exasperating route once before? More familiar sights welcomed me at the hospital. I nodded knowingly to the Blessed Mother, still serenely maintaining her vigil. I didn't slow my advance, knowing the hated "take-a-number machine" and triage awaited.

Number in hand (thankfully acquired without incident or line crashers), I began my customary pacing, huffing, and grimacing in the hospital lobby with furious intensity. I was worried that an administrative lag would brand me as a blacklisted debtor, a claim I was prepared to rebut with the copy of the settlement I had packed in my hospital bag. If necessary, I was prepared to summon the full force of my maternal protective instincts, then operating at ACTIVE LABOR LEVEL NEUROTIC! Simultaneously, these same instincts flooded my cerebrum with shrill bulletins "Get to a doctor! Get to a doctor!" and "Mayday! Mayday! Mayday!"—a message reinforced by the severity of my contractions.

The full force of my concern narrowed to seeing a doctor when Josh trotted back from reception triumphantly reporting we were cleared for admittance. Sadly, my power was limited to attempting to summon my number by directing an anguish-fueled laser stare at the screen on which it was eventually to appear.

A doctor finally called us to an examination room. As I had suspected, I was too far along to have to even consider asinine suggestions of a C-section. Instead, the nurses immediately began mobilizing for relocation to the birthing room, starting with their cruel policy of hijacking husbands to scrub in during their wives' hour of peril.

So consumed by the pain, I was only dimly conscious of happenings outside my body. An abandoned seal beached on the examination table, I thrashed about scared and barked for rescue: "Drugs pleeeeaase!" The staff kept to their preparations, engaging me only with the occasional question. I eventually surmised that their desire to know my weight was linked to their ability to administer the correct dosage of that magic medication. I switched tactics to pleading for a smartphone to make a pound to kilo conversion, my Yankee upbringing having left me a metric system illiterate. Alas, my spasmodic dribbles of the Portuguese language that emerged between contractions did not represent intelligible speech, much less an adequate explanation of my bizarre request for a smartphone; perhaps they thought I wanted to take a labor selfie? Experienced in the role of misunderstood misfit, I knew my efforts to be futile and resigned myself to my latest failure of situational competency. Lacking other resources on which to draw, I withdrew to contend with the struggle raging within.

Still only vaguely aware of my environment, I was rolled through halls and up the elevator to a birthing room, perking up only to the ringing directive, "She needs an epidural yesterday!" An anesthesiologist soon arrived and instructed, "Ma'am, we need you to sit." Nodding, I attempted to comply only to find the task impossible given the immense propulsive force then shooting out my hind end. Looking up helplessly, the anesthesiologist firmly reiterated, "We cannot administer the drug unless you are seated." Nodding again, I summoned my desperation's full resolve to temporarily quash the propulsion, assuming a precarious but qualifying sitting position.

The debilitating pain subsided and I awoke to my environment. I saw the medical team poised for action at the foot of my bed. Josh, scrubbed and ready, rejoined the scope of my consciousness. He whispered to me that we had spoiled our obstetrician's evening plans; the advanced state of my labor had forced her to extend her shift. Studying her face, I found it utterly unfamiliar despite our time together. Was she the same doctor who had called us to the examination room? In the fog of pain, I had no idea. Regardless, I silently prayed for the best under her care.

"Push!" the doctor directed. I gathered my strength for what I assumed would be a laborious final stretch. When, only a few pushes later, the obstetrician announced the baby's arrival, my first thought was, "Already?!" The clock pointed to just before midnight, about four hours since we had left home.

Within minutes my baby peacefully rested in my arms, and I basked in the pure sweetness of the moment. Josh took this turn, making his now traditional introduction, "Hi, I'm Daddy." Then he added, "And you're Gabriel."

It was time to move to the baby resort. My memories of the nurses and their competent care brought peaceful anticipation. En route, Gabriel let out a wail, and I instinctively prepared for 10 rounds of divining what might soothe him. Much to my surprise, he nestled into my chest and returned to sleep. I had imagined such a moment would be possible before Nicolas' harrowing newborn days; what could a baby find more comforting than a mother's embrace? But I had long since filed the notion under silly ideas I used to believe until life's hard knocks showed me different. I had not anticipated the arrival of an angelic snuggler, easily calmed. This child was quieted by the sonority of my beating heart, and I breathlessly gave thanks for happy surprises.

16

PECULIAR MADEMOISELLE

Having completed the trek up the long, sloping incline that took my boys, our mammoth stroller, and me home from our neighborhood park, I paused to catch my breath. I saw a delivery truck park at the local bakery, and I recognized the driver. The lyrics to "Belle" from Disney's *Beauty and the Beast* flashed in my head:

Little town
It's a quiet village
Every day
Like the one before
Little town
Full of little people
Waking up to say
Bonjour bonjour
Bonjour bonjour bonjour

I had been playing this song at home, along with other Disney classics, as part of my efforts to teach my children aspects of American culture they would not naturally absorb growing up in Brazil.

"Belle" and the opening to *The Lion King's* "Circle of Life" (TAA DA DAT DA DAA!!!) often gave me the *umph* I needed to tackle the dishes. Thank you, Mr. Disney. Sharing my initiative with my sister, she chided me for preparing my kids to meet the challenges of American social interactions with pop culture knowledge decades behind the times. "What about *Moana* and *Frozen*?" she asked.

Sighing, I leaned in to restart forward motion, wondering how much longer I could support my load, physical and otherwise. In addition to large strollers, I had recently been weighed down by the fear of my own irrelevance. For almost two years now I had spent the majority of my days within a stroller-friendly radius of our apartment. Limited by these parameters, I could not claim to participate in the excitement possible in this city—that which had motivated my decision to relocate, now years ago and seemingly far away. I was not gaining "unique experience" to establish myself as a corruption expert. My days of catching a last-minute flight to Rio de Janeiro faded to memory. Even more faded were my memories of New York, bursting out of Grand Central Station, fierce in my black trench coat and patent leather heels, a social life that involved cocktail and dinner parties. Now I habitually walked the same quiet São Paulo sidewalks, my tots in tow, sporting mom uniform essentials: a "yet another bad hair day" baseball hat and a "hand-free" backpack handbag. I had mommy wrist, stroller back, and a hand rash from washing after every diaper change.

Stopping again at a red light, my thoughts tormented me: "What further proof do you need of your own insignificance? Your predictable little life has you on a face recognition basis with a neighborhood delivery man." I had no rebuttal as I pushed on to the final stretch, toward home, nodding as I went to the taxi drivers at their post, engaged in their usual pleasant idleness, seemingly oblivious to a world that had long since moved on to smartphone ride-hailing apps.

I gloomily recalled another recent reminder of my own insignificance. On my first day back at work after maternity leave, I had attended a luncheon at which my alma mater, University of Notre Dame, gave its highest honor to Judge Sérgio Moro for showing "exemplary dedication to the ideals for which the University stands: faith, inquiry, education, justice, public service, peace, and care of the most vulnerable." Since I had left the Petrobras project, the judge's efforts had seen the former president of Brazil jailed for corruption, an event unprecedented in the country's history. Regarding the judge as a shining example of what I had once dreamed of accomplishing, yet now saw no path to achieve, angst tinged my heartfelt congratulations.

My life had become so predictable it dulled the pain of my stress. When summer brought yet another tropical disease outbreak, yellow fever, I dutifully rubbed the industrial strength repellent into Gabriel's tender skin, his infant body not yet eligible for vaccination. When I received news that monkeys had been found dead from the disease at the U.S. Consulate, where I had not long before presented Gabriel for his documentation, I exhaled a sigh of rueful helplessness. And when I again traded the challenges of flying solo with kids in exchange for extra time with distant family, I rolled through travel's hurdles feeling as though I were simply reenacting a scene I had rehearsed ad nauseam.

Back at our apartment, I wearily chased down little hands to wash and little shoes to remove, routine work incapable of distracting me from my sullen musings: "Who was I but just another funny character in my own provincial town? The peculiar mademoiselle herself!" The song's lyrics resumed in my head:

Look there she goes the girl is strange, but special
A most peculiar mademoiselle!
It's a pity as a sin
She doesn't quite fit in
'Cause she really is a funny girl

I was surely cast for the role. The neighborhood had few foreigners, and my accent gave me away whenever I spoke Portuguese. Such was my plight as an adult language learner: I was a perpetual curiosity who never truly grasped the subjunctive tense. The best compliment on my proficiency I could hope for was "Are you from Portugal?" It was like living with a bright red clown nose affixed to my face, inspiring a sly "there is something funny about you" smile from everyone I encountered—with the particularly curious inevitably venturing, "So, where are you from?"

I was tired. Tired of always being the oddity who inspired polite, but probing questions. Tired of not having shared experiences that would foster intimate friendships. Tired of not having the language finesse to orchestrate complex activity. And most of all, tired of being on the outside.

Yet, I knew I could expect little change to my circumstances, outside of the continual threat of an abrupt, dramatic exodus in the event of a company bankruptcy. Trapped in the tropics, how could I contemplate writing "S.O.S" in the sand when rescue would mean failure and financial disaster for my family?

My boys loaded in their highchairs and lunch served, I paused again, wistfully staring out the laundry room window at my neighborhood fiefdom below, wondering if the big, wonderful possibilities I used to imagine for my contributions to the world were dreams as dated as my Disney playlists.

My insecurities continued to churn during nap time, the hour's quiet melancholy forced reckoning with a reality I was loath to admit: I could perhaps tolerate my professional shortcomings if I at least felt as though I were succeeding in my revised, little mission. I had thought

I could not fail, but the challenges of motherhood seemed to have multiplied disproportionately with the addition of one angelic child. Josh was working harder than ever, even forgetting my birthday during a particularly hectic period. (His futile attempt at defense? "But I only forgot it in the morning!") When I reluctantly signed off on a "four or five day" trip for Josh to court investors, I was horrified to see his final itinerary spanned nine nights, representing a disastrous miscommunication between mom and CEO priority metrics: solo dinners/bedtimes versus business days away from the office. Nicolas' intense persona magnified the toddler moments natural to his age and daily stretched my patience. And Gabriel, while supremely easygoing, was still a helpless, tiny human dependent on me for care. I was too often a frazzled, irritable overseer of chaos and squawks rather than the zen, present mother of the park.

One tactic I employed to avoid joining in on the screaming was singing a rousing, punctuated version of "Row, row, row your boat," finding the melody well-suited to channel frustration. But in more enlightened moments, I sought to summon the Blessed Mother's emergency intervention on the hot mess *du jour*, singing one of my favorite hymns: "Gentle woman, quiet light, morning star, so strong and bright, gentle Mother, peaceful dove, teach us wisdom; teach us love." Gritting my teeth as I sang, I felt myself far from the ideal of gentle, peaceful, and wise.

This day's confrontations confirmed a feeling long brewing. I needed a new outlook, and new coping techniques, to find peace in my intractable circumstances. Humbled again by my perceived failure, I offered up a tearful prayer; "Dear Lord. Maybe achieving my highest and best use is useless. But at least I don't want to mess up the lot I have. Help me show love to my family. Help me be a light."

17

FIAT

Sitting against the washing machine, my head slumped between my knees, I sobbed uncontrollably. Closed-in on one side by a window view of my neighborhood confines and on the other my kitchen battleground, a glass sliding door semi-shielding me from the children I feared failing, I surrendered to the despair that had been building.

We had just returned from our annual summer trip to the U.S., characterized by flashes of enjoyment between grueling feats of endurance. The month leading up to our trip had seen every weekend consumed by trials instead of the usual activities we, like many families, relied on and desperately needed to recharge.

First came the stomach flu, mercifully slaying me first and permitting a partial recovery before I had to stand watch over my sick boys, Josh included. Possessing only a wisp of returning strength, I administered fluids and changed soiled sheets. I hardly minded when my children, seeking comfort in the arms of their mother, threw up on me instead of the floor, couch, or bed. It took far less of my precious energy to take a shower than to scrub the vomit's other random targets.

In hot pursuit of that ordeal came unending solo parenting while Josh oversaw two major moves at the company. Its size now requiring a separate office and warehouse; sales were growing even as Josh continued to struggle to attract investment. As B2B distributor, it aspired to sell anything a company might need, meaning it had to store a tremendous diversity of product—from paperclips to cleaning supplies to forklifts. Just as entrepreneurial life had demanded his wearing company paramedic and firefighter hats among others, here, too, necessity required his performance of unconventional labors for the executive. During the weekend warehouse move, he joined the team in an intense, physical hustle, scrambling to get 80 semi-trucks of inventory in place before sales resumed on Monday. In the comparatively tame office move, unexpected and often-mundane tasks still managed to ensnare him for long hours, such as scrambling to install toilet paper dispensers mysteriously absent in all bathrooms.

Our summer trip to the United States gave us a chance to extract ourselves from a dark month that had offered us no respite.

We first traveled to South Bend for our 10-year Notre Dame reunion, and I reentered a community fabric beloved by the university's students, faculty, and alumni. Encapsulating this aura, former university President Father Hesburgh remarked at one commencement: "Let us agree that we shall never forget one another. And whatever happens, let us remember how good it felt when we were all here together united by a good and decent feeling, which made us better people—better probably than we would otherwise have ever been." Accustomed to operating on subsistence level social support and emotional fumes, I had, indeed, forgotten how good I felt in the embrace of high-octane community that made us all better people. Waves of remembrances inundated me throughout the weekend. When I joined my classmates in singing lyrics we had sung at every dorm Mass we had attended as students—"Peace I leave with you my friends, my friends for I am with you til the end"—my lost sense of belonging definitively rekindled.

We traveled next to my native Minnesota, where the simple pleasures of an all-American summer greeted me. Enjoying lawn chair happy hours with my family, watching my children romp in the water sprinkler with their cousins and play with heirloom tricycles and Tonka trucks, I continued to recover my depleted strength. I inhaled with a rarefied appreciation the commonplace sights of my youth: Americana red barns and rolling fields brightly framed by cumulus clouds afloat in an idyllic blue sky, sparkling lakes, and lazy sunsets.

Ironically, it was precisely my exceptional enjoyment of the trip that tipped me over the edge of despair and onto the laundry room floor after our return to Brazil. The vacation's end plopped me right back on a treadmill of challenges; overdue potty training, an empty fridge, full laundry baskets, all demanding my attention. Confronted with these challenges, my mighty internal drive stalled, overcome by the vicious return of my lonely existence. In the intensely familiar scenes of my domesticity, I only saw what was absent: the euphoria possible in the embrace of community and family. My recent, tantalizing brush with its flame now harshly extinguished, I stared down a future that seemed endlessly dark—and I lacked all resolve to carry on. Years of Herculean get up and go were diminished to complete paralysis. Hopeless, I choked out another tear-stained prayer: "Dear Lord. Please pick me up. I have a family to take care of."

The next day saw me slowly, haltingly running in my beloved park. A prayer answered, I found myself tentatively upright and capable of forward motion. Progressing along my familiar track, I ran in awe of the grace that allowed this small victory, knowing my own strength would have left me a puddle on the laundry room floor. Running, running, one question burned in my mind, "How can I get more of this magic elixir, grace?"

Finishing my run, I sat on a bench, hoping to unjumble my thoughts under the inspiration of the park's verdant canopy. Having survived both a brush with collapse and the other side's wobbly first steps, I was firmly resolved on one thing: I would definitively reevaluate the way I understood the world. The way I had been operating had proved catastrophically ineffective and my well-being demanded a better strategy.

Desperate to hasten myself to a safer distance from the dark hole I had recently escaped, I crumbled again into tears, realizing I was clueless about how to begin, how to build on the feelings of small victory the run had engendered. How to recapture at least some of the euphoria of the visit to the U.S. Then I decided to search "chronic loneliness" on my phone, chiding myself for reaching yet another new low: sobbing in a public place while seeking solace in a medium as impersonal as internet self-help.

Adrift again in darkness, I sat upright to a piercing realization, an epiphany gleaned from the garbled expert analyses that danced in my head: I would always be lonely if I were not brave enough to show others the parts of myself I believed to be weak, quirky, or unlikeable. This assertion seemed noncontroversial, perhaps even obvious. Yet as I turned it over in my mind I readily acknowledged I did not champion vulnerability. True, I had tired of the invincibility learned from my Manhattan education, yet my social reflex remained one of armament or avoidance. I had only come to enjoy that "good and decent feeling" at Notre Dame after friendly overtures soothed a tempest of insecurities I had whipped up imagining the reunion as a 10-year achievement check-in and corresponding judgement. And I had run egged on by the desire to fix all my issues before I messed up my kids.

Nourished with this crumb of revelation, I stood up to return home, apprehensive, yet curious about the journey ahead.

18

BATTLE LINES

Back at the park later that week, I pushed my tot-laden stroller up the sloping incline of the park's far edge. As I leaned in to scale the hill, I smiled, enjoying both the day and the recollection of my latest epiphany.

I sought to invite both grace and understanding by committing to a daily regimen of spiritual inspiration. It seemed a considerably better approach than doing things like searching "chronic loneliness" on my phone. Consequently, I had signed up to follow different online resources. Through one, I had found an article that contrasted acceptance with resignation when responding to difficulties.[6] In Fr. Jacques Philippe's *Interior Freedom*, he suggested that affirmatively accepting our difficulties transforms their nature by fully entrusting them to God. Alternatively, passive resignation leaves us to tolerate life and its problems the best we can.

Fresh from facing down despair, I could easily recognize my go-to tactics — "beat it down" and if that doesn't work, "grin and bear it" — as failed strategies. I wondered if it were only by abandoning my usual coping techniques that I had opened myself up to the grace of my miraculous rise from the laundry room floor. Perhaps in my abject helplessness God had given me credit for a de facto, beginner's acceptance? Having survived a look into the abyss, I already felt a strange new peace with the prospect of continued expat life and loneliness. While the hurt remained, I found comfort knowing that, through God's grace, it could not defeat me.

I marveled at the wildly radical nature of the suggested replacement. I best knew a world that demanded effort until we effected the change we desired. Go, go, go. Never would I have considered declaring "let it be done" as a possible best course of action.

Unloading Nicolas and Gabriel at our destination, I mused how my life could change with a stronger commitment to a practice of acceptance. I whispered, "*Okay,* I live abroad. *Okay,* friends and family dear to me are far away. *Okay,* I'll quit fighting this. Help me accept my situation."

Another day in the still unfolding world on the other side of broken, I woke early. The house was quiet so I lingered, reluctant to rise. True to my resolution, I woke each morning determined to find my new north. While some days I felt myself benevolently guided along the providential points of illumination, just as often I thrashed about in dark uncertainty, still woefully lacking the principles to position me firmly upright. I felt at one moment full of enlightenment and hope and then, in another, unrest and angst. Attempting to explain myself to my perplexed husband, I could only remark that I felt myself on a drawn-out journey to breakdown or breakthrough. What would today bring? I closed my eyes, confronting newly revealed battle lines.

I had not stopped wondering why I still seemed so perilously close to crumbling even as grace and acceptance had begun to remove the debilitating power of loneliness. If I could not blame my perennial thorn, what then was causing my continued turmoil? Then this rumination, raw and determined, spit out an uncomfortable truth: I did not feel deserving of love.

Reflecting on my past, I easily discerned achievement as the source of my insecurity. "Do" had always been my lynchpin verb, driving my evolving ambitions as well as the near-constant analysis that ran in my head, assessing the most productive use of any minute. Only now could I see what I had been blind to before: I had been scrambling to *earn love*. The true motivation lurking behind my efforts was an attempt to earn my worth. "You are only as valuable as your achievements" was the pernicious soundtrack of my subconscious. When my efforts collided with failure, I naturally fell into the snares of despair.

I could also see now that this collision had been long in the making. First, New York's ethos spiked my innate ambition, and I equated my vocation with achievement. Next, I moved abroad, in part, with the aim of improving my chances of high-caliber achievement. Once abroad, I found my efforts hampered by an environment I was ill-suited to navigate, fueling frustration. Then embracing motherhood, I distanced myself from a career-oriented success, yet my original North Star—using my talents to their highest and best use—remained intact. Finally, the challenges of motherhood proved better suited to acquaint me with my limitations rather than my achievements. Throughout my young adult life I had maintained an unhealthy and uneasy relationship with achievement.

Opening my eyes, I reeled. The entire foundation on which I had ordered my life had proven faulty. I required so much more than a few new coping techniques. On what—if anything—did I stand? How should I proceed? Desperate for solid ground, I mentally pulled up a theology primer ingrained from my years of Catholic school.

"God is love" and "Jesus loves us."

The statements almost rang with the irrelevance of cliché, such had they been repeated to me since childhood. Then there was the more substantive theology from my high school classes.

"We have inherent dignity because God made us in his image and likeness."

"Humans are good, but inclined toward evil as a result of original sin."

"Jesus saved us through His passion, death, and resurrection."

Last, I remembered a college theology class that introduced me to the Catholic Church's understanding of the role of our actions. It was here that I first learned that grace, freely given by God, is necessary for any good action on our part. And even when moved by this celestial pixie dust, we can never achieve merit equal to the gift of our salvation. I recalled finding the whole lesson rather odd. Before this class I had assumed maintaining a certain threshold of good deeds was the determining factor for salvation. Perhaps subconsciously, I had even thought there must have been some mistake. No one had mentioned the inadequacy of human action in my many previous years of religious education. At the very least, I was not sure it mattered. Achievement, regardless of its motivation, surely remained the goal. Was it not toward this end that all these educational institutions sought to hone my skills and intellect? Besides, the details of this grace paradigm seemed slippery, impervious to precise calculation. Certainly it was safer just to be really awesome to ensure I made the heavenly cut.

And now, wallowing in my failures of achievement and charity, I finally had to reckon with these archived academic tenets. No longer distanced by the airy confidence of youth and the veneer of academic debate, I squirmed, considering their implications for my life here and now.

Jesus loves us—loves me—so much he assured our salvation by submitting himself to a horrendous death on a cross, enduring every type of evil and indignity in the process. Impaired by original sin and my human nature, I could never hope to repay this debt, giving me no other option but to accept with humility this great gift. My inherent dignity also resulted from purely divine action: being made in the image and likeness of God. Together these divine actions offered an unexpected answer to the question of both my worth and my fate: God rendered them both a non-issue by freely bestowing me with His own stainless dignity and allowing His only Son to die for my sins.

"What an incredibly uncomfortable proposition," I mused, exhaling my discomfort.

My Minnesota manners dictated I reject a host's offer of a glass of water at least several times before accepting to avoid inconveniencing him or her. Yet in the love on offer by Jesus, I have to have the gall to accept gifts of ultimate importance *and* accept that I have no ability to pay Him back. No wonder I had long avoided facing this reality, so egregious was the imbalance. It had seemed preferable, prudent or polite even, to earn my own keep. Or, easier to assume I was not loved when bested by my insecurities.

Insecurity. I felt its weight on me now. I heard it whispering to me to reject God's offer as too good to be true, perhaps even a trick. Maybe meant for other, better people but certainly not for me. Sure, I could intellectually accept all I had learned in my classes as true. Yet I still worried. Was it a problem that I *felt* so miserably unloved and unworthy? If so, how could I untwist knots rooted so deep? Although on a journey of spiritual understanding, I felt physical tightness in my chest, the sensation that my heart was being forcefully molded anew. Would I finally arrive at a breakdown or breakthrough? I could not be sure. But I held a quiet hope that it would be the latter.

Finally getting out of bed, I silently pleaded for serenity.

19

PETALS AND *MERDA*

I felt free! For the first time in a long time I didn't feel the tightness in my chest!" I jubilantly reported to my high school friends via a video messaging app.

I had just returned from an hour spent outside playing with my boys. Responding to their infectious enthusiasm, I temporarily escaped my gloomy world and lost myself in their bright one. They chased balls with a furious intensity and then lingered over a discovered treasure. They attempted heroic new playground feats and then believed a kiss could heal any ouchie.

The past week I had asked my friends for their advice on my latest quandary: how to connect my head and my heart in believing God's love for me. Their advice was unanimous. I needed to practice gratitude. Thus, I had spent the week scribbling in a notebook such blessings as boisterous boys full of life, kitchen dance parties, park expeditions, clean laundry, and hot coffee. Unsurprisingly, my mood lifted. When I recalled how much I delighted in my children's ability to endlessly enjoy the park's rocks, sticks, and leaves, I chided myself for ever having taken my everyday blessings for granted.

My notebook had become a lifeline as I continued to emerge from my hole. It was a means to identify new blessings at the slightest hint of melancholy, to organize my scattered thoughts around principles capable of rooting me firmly upright, and most recently, to record memories. These recorded memories served as the basis of a new project I had decided to undertake: giving formal expression to the episodes, decisive and poignant, that had shaped my adult existence. At first I questioned the value of this project. Surely, I knew my own story and it would be of little interest to anyone else. "It's a waste of time!" I would chastise myself. Though I persisted in deference to a hodgepodge of factors. There is the quiet, but insistent whisper present in every human heart to be creative and to connect with others. I reasoned writing was a more stimulating and productive use of my precious free time than scanning social media or shopping online. And most unequivocally, when I asked my sad, pitiful reflection in a mirror how I might find a way out of my present darkness, a voice in my head encouraged, "Write!"

Hearing this command startled me. First, I knew it to have arisen from outside myself, even as I heard it in my own head. It was not an idea I would have ever thought of on my own. I had not before received such an explicit directive of mysterious origin. It was not an aggressive command; it was more like a friend exhorting me to do the obvious thing that would make me better. Second, writing seemed as plausible for me, a Type A accountant, as learning to fly. Yet, at the same time, it was an idea that made perfect sense. I had enjoyed composing little stories as a child and had leveraged writing as cheap therapy during my angsty teenager times. Why not pick up writing again now? I walked away from that mirror encouraged, confident I had received another crumb to guide me on my journey.

I finished my message to my friends by thanking them for their advice. Then I immediately grabbed my notebook to add new entries of gratitude: Gabriel's determination and a clover bouquet from Nicolas.

"Everything is grace."[7] Later that week I was perusing the day's spiritual guidance when the quote jumped out from the computer screen and poked me. It was attributed to St. Thérèse of Lisieux, whose autobiography, *Story of a Soul*, I had just reread. St. Thérèse was a cloistered Carmelite nun in 19th century France who died of tuberculosis at only 24. Fond of floral imagery, she encouraged souls to do little things with great love, proclaiming, "If every tiny flower wanted to be a rose, spring would lose its loveliness."[8] While she died in near obscurity, posthumously her writings became popular, even earning her the title of Doctor of the Church, a distinction given to those saints who have made a significant contribution to theology. I had decided to reread her book—the first time I read it was when I was a teenager—because I vaguely recalled her advice about a "little way" and hoped it would help me find solace in my own little world.

In her declaration—"No other means have I of proving my love than to strew flowers; that is, to let no little sacrifice escape me, not a look, not a word, to avail of the very least actions and do them for Love…not one shall I find without shedding its petals for Thee."—I saw an inspired mindset capable of tackling drudgery with magnanimity.[9] "Leave no flower unstrewn!" I would silently exhort myself, facing my own petals: yet another blowout, meltdown, meal prep, or Josh's errant socks.

What, then, did this saintly master of the mundane mean when she proclaimed *everything* is grace? Grace, that magical pixie dust necessary for any good action on our part, is formally defined as "the free and undeserved help that God gives us to respond to his call to become children of God, adoptive sons, partakers of the divine nature, and of eternal life."[10] If we profess "everything is grace," we understand every moment and aspect of our life to be a gift from God—specifically tailored to help us in our faith journey and deserving of our gratitude. *Every* moment and aspect. I did not see any disclaimer, so I could only assume St. Thérèse meant including the crappy ones. And there, she lost me. "Why?" I chafed. "Why should I give thanks for life's *merda?*"

Rumblings of this question first emerged when my friends advised me to practice gratitude. One of my friends shared a quote by St. Paul: "Have no anxiety at all, but in *everything*, by prayer and petition, with thanksgiving, make your requests known to God."[11] Gung ho on gratitude, I picked up *One Thousand Gifts*, a New York Times best seller on the topic. I experienced visceral chagrin when I read the author's assertion that worrying is practical atheism.[12] I had never before understood my time-honored pastime as an affront to my believer status. And now St. Thérèse, my new favorite saint, added her "Everything is grace" poke to the mix.

The unanimity of these intellectual and spiritual pinpricks demanded I revisit my response to hardship. I understood good and bad were distinct forces pitted against each other. I had learned only God was capable of the act of creation, hence evil was always a corruption of the good. Yes, there was redemptive suffering, a stoic "offering it up" of life's misfortunes to provide some vague assistance in the divine plan, but I had never taken this to mean that I should be thankful for that which was bad.

Yet I could concede I may have missed something. The stabilizing principles I was seeking would be incomplete without a credible response to life's difficulties. My scars and sins knew I could document warm fuzzies all day long, only to be overcome by *merda* and petals. St. Thérèse's quote still lingered on my screen. I clicked around, a mindless search to avoid a difficult question. Then, much to my surprise, the answer emerged from another page: "Out of the darkness is born the light."[13]

Out of darkness, light. Out of the bad, good. I knew this phenomenon to be true from my own experience. Through my new writing project, I had reviewed plagues of biblical proportions that I had survived: fly babies, lethal mosquitos, dead monkeys, shifty birth plans, and the company's quarterly flirtations with bankruptcy. In all these I brought my prescribed M.O. for tough times: crippling worry and a dogged, futile search for control. Not once in any of these hardships did I consider there might be an easier, better way to respond. When finally I asked God to make me not such a miserable mess, I was made an even more miserable mess, subject to the darkest moments of my life puddled on the laundry room floor.

But now, having just survived this darkness, I could already marvel at the mastery of the divine hand in responding to my prayer. When I considered my impressive obstinacy in the face of every other hardship—my heart harder than Pharaoh's—I saw how I left God no choice but to cut me down at my weakest spots: my family and my sense of belonging. And administer the decisive blow He did, mercifully leveling me so I might finally let Him guide me along a new path. While I was still emerging, I was already breathing easier, metaphorically and literally, as long and slow inhales and exhales eased the tightness in my chest.

So, yes, I could understand giving thanks for petals and *merda*. But could I trust Him in any and all darkness? While abhorrent to think about truly awful hypotheticals, I was committed to finding an answer to any question that arose on this journey. Would I still welcome the workings of His hand in a confirmed case of Zika, actual bankruptcy, or an as-yet unknown tragedy?

I did not doubt that God was all-powerful, all-knowing, and

all-loving. I accepted that in allowing us free will He also allowed us the ability to make an awful mess of His creation, starting in the Garden of Eden. I believed God's involvement in humanity ultimately a rescue effort—and the Bible a tale of salvation history. In the Old Testament, God established covenant after promise, sent prophet after prophet, all in an effort to help us remedy our own messes. In the New Testament, God took our messes entirely on Himself with the uncomfortably generous sacrifice of His only Son, who confronted every evil to pay our debt in full. God, then, is fully capable of bringing good out of evil. Once more, the good He draws is greater than had the evil never existed. God took our sins and transformed them into the greatest act of human love and the great hope of humanity. That is quite a significant upgrade!

But to accept *my* sufferings, actual and hypothetical, as under God's mysterious, benevolent stewardship, I had to believe He loved *me*. Not only in a sound theoretical, lofty theological way, but in a personal, passionate, tenderly caring for me in every moment with the earnest intention of bringing me home safely at the end of my days kind of way.

Had I been able to make my heart feel what my head knew, that God loved me? The lie—that He did not love me or that His love was contingent on my performance—once exposed, had lost much of its efficacy. Once exposed, I was aghast that I had unwittingly been led to believe this, the devil's linchpin lie. So while still hurting, searching, healing, I was eager to dispel the pernicious whispers of my unworthiness and wholly believe.

Inhaling, I mentally resolved, "Okay. From now on, everything is grace."

20

LESSONS IN LITTER

I stared in anguish at a plastic wrapper mixed among fallen foliage at the park. Only an unassuming bit of litter, it had ignited a burning dilemma: *to pick it up or not to pick it up?*

I had recently listened to a homily that upended my thinking on achievement.[14] Preaching on St. Paul's letters to the Ephesians—"He chose us in Him, before the foundation of the world, to be holy and without blemish before Him"—Bishop Robert Barron asserted that God's choice of us is vastly more important than any of our choices.[15] Consequently, he explained, we should follow God's plan for us, which by no means must conform to our expectations. When we choose to adhere to divine will over our personal prerogatives, we fulfill our roles in the Theo-Drama, God's master plan of salvation. Alternatively, we live in an Ego-Drama when we prioritize our own aspirations and plans. Concluding, Bishop Baron promised that our roles in the Theo-Drama are infinitely grander and more exciting than any of our own making. Indeed, one ordained before the dawn of creation.

Do God's will. Not a terribly revolutionary directive for those who believe. Yet hearing it presented in this manner—God's plan as supremely wiser than my own ideas and initiatives—gave me tremendous peace. Since my station in life had taken a sharp, humbling turn, my achievement-fueled insecurities had simmered in subversive dissatisfaction. While confident in my vocation as a mother, I was not sure spending my days fully engaged in what could be viewed as tedious non-accomplishment constituted my highest and best use. In my cynical self-analysis, a life spent endlessly wiping the bottoms and noses of my own kin was a self-serving feat of endurance, not altruism. Even as my reality consistently showed I lacked spare capacity, I would still think, "Shouldn't I be doing something more, something *exceptional*?"

The importance of God's will over our own, so unequivocally stated, soothed my frenzied ambition and gave me permission to relax in the knowledge that faithfully fulfilling my "peculiar mademoiselle" and "mother hen" roles *did* represent my best contribution to the world. It was a tender whisper from God: "You are right where you need to be. I chose it just for you." Freed from naysaying doubts, I was ready to take up the vocation of my little world with renewed zeal.

And then my overthinking, productivity-driven brain went off and confused my resolve.

Gabriel was in full inquisitive toddlerhood. Recently, he had begun exploring the world by attempting to sample trash. My annoyance fueled an idea: I could pick up litter while my kids played. The park's relative downtime and the near-empty plastic bag I had taken to carrying for trash that struck Gabriel's fancy begged me to use them. The moment I started this practice, however, I lost sight of the park I loved, an oasis of toodle time and tranquility. Instead, I saw only offensive litter blots. Fuming, I would spew judgment on those park goers, so lazy and disrespectful, that they chose to litter rather than put their trash in one of the many, many receptacles available. In the heights of my high-mindedness, I imagined a city-wide campaign with shame-inducing placards; "Hey, you! Yeah, you! Don't leave trash for my baby to eat!"

Then, thankfully, grace checked my indignation. I wondered, "Was this a really good idea? Or just my insecurities again trying to aggrandize the world that I had just resolved to embrace as is?" Having just chucked my lifelong understanding of right action, my industrious core whirred in nervous confusion. Helpless, even somewhat paralyzed, I could only stare down at the trash: *to pick it up or not to pick it up?*

In the afternoon's calm I sat with my copy of *Story of a Soul.* I was clearly in need of revisiting the fundamentals of St. Thérèse's little way. Trash patrol, surely among the more elementary acts of service, should not cause such consternation. I located the chapter containing her petal primer and began reading:

> To be your Spouse, to be a Carmelite, and by my union with You to be Mother of Souls, should not suffice me? And yet it is not so. No doubt these three privileges sum up my true vocation: Carmelite, Spouse, Mother, and yet I feel within me other vocations. I feel the vocation of THE WARRIOR, THE PRIEST, THE APOSTLE, THE DOCTOR, THE MARTYR. Finally I feel the need and desire of carrying out the most heroic deeds for You, O Jesus."[16]

I was firmly established in a vocation that had been a dream since youth, yet I was restless for grander achievements. Yep, that sounded familiar. I saw my own epitaph varying only slightly: Spouse, Mother, and Neighborhood Eccentric.

> O Jesus…How can I combine these contrasts? How can I realize the desires of my poor little soul?[17]

Check and check. How many times had I tried to devise an exit from my isolated, irrelevant state without success? How often had my plans of great benevolence collided with my shortcomings?

Resolute in her search for what constitutes the best, most heroic acts, St. Thérèse turned to the writings of the apostle, martyr, and Christianity's foremost evangelist, St. Paul. At first she finds little comfort in his proclamation that "not all can be apostles, prophets, and doctors."[18] But enticed by his promise—"And yet I will show you a more excellent way"—she read on to his most renowned verse:

> If I speak in human and angelic tongues but do not have love, I am a resounding gong or clashing cymbal. And if I have the gift of prophecy and comprehend all mysteries and all knowledge; if I have all faith so as to move mountains but do not have love, I am nothing.
>
> Love is patient, love is kind. It is not jealous, is not pompous, is not inflated, is not rude, it does not seek its own interests, it is not quick-tempered, it does not brood over injury, it does not rejoice over wrongdoing but rejoices with the truth. It bears all things, believes all things, hopes all things endures all things.[19]

Upon reading "the most PERFECT gifts are nothing without love" and "Charity is the EXCELLENT WAY that leads most surely to God" St. Thérèse cried out, "my vocation, at last I have found it… MY VOCATION IS LOVE."[20]

Love as "the most excellent way," a truth about which believers and non-believers could agree. It was the practical application with which we all struggled. Endless patience? Consistent kindness? The ability to endure all things? I could sooner rid the world of corruption or the park of trash than flawlessly practice this virtue. Adding to my frustration, I had recently read a reflection that said accepting God's love was necessary to be able to share it with others. Having recently realized I struggled with accepting God's lavishly generous, saving love, this assertion irked me. I ruefully wondered if I would ever be able to affect any genuine good, much less apply myself to my highest and best use.

"What would St. Therese tell me?" I thought. Reflecting on the entirety of her writings, I took heart. I recalled how she frequently wrote of her own limitations, suggesting doubt was also a topic that also occupied her thoughts. She regularly compared herself to a child—little, powerless, and weak.[21] As a child, she confessed to having had trouble understanding theology, explaining herself, and performing great deeds; she might even fall asleep in God's presence.[22] Yet time and time again she refused to be discouraged, answering her doubts with the insight that made her one of the most celebrated saints of modern times. She understood that our weakness can be strength to the extent it inspires us to allow God to work in us.

In the petal primer she again doubted herself—"I am the smallest of creatures; I know my misery and my feebleness"— and again overcame her doubt with hope.[23] Having declared herself capable of showing her love only by "strewing flowers," she was confident in the efficacy of her small sacrifices. She wrote:

> O Jesus, of what use will my little flowers be to You? Ah! I know very well that this fragrant shower, the fragile, worthless petals...will charm You. Yes, these nothings will please you. They will bring a smile to the Church Triumphant. She will gather up my flowers unpetalled *through love* and have them pass through Your own divine hands, O Jesus. And this Church in heaven, desirous of playing

> with her little child, will cast these flowers, which are now infinitely valuable because of Your divine touch…upon the Church…in order to gain victory for it.[24]

Yes, St. Thérèse had her doubts, but they did not cause her to fear her weakness. What then was I missing? What did I still need to understand to shed my fear of weakness? Then it clicked. While I ascribed to God the same calculating mentality that torments human interactions as mundane as accepting a glass of water, she praised the abundance of His mercy. Necessary to St. Thérèse's unconventional worldview—weakness as a source of strength—was her firm conviction that even as we forever fail to love, God's love is perfect. His love is endlessly patient, consistently kind, and can endure all things. It is all that St. Paul proclaimed and no doubt, even better still. In our imperfect humanity, we can only imperfectly understand or express the magnificence of God's love. What can you do in the face of such love? Come as you are. Humbly offer Him your best efforts *and* epic fails. Just as a child can be confident of a parent's love and support even as they cannot understand, explain, perform, or even stay awake, we can be confident of God's love.

What then did all this mean for me? Accepting God's love was necessary to achieve my aim, but not in the way I had imagined.

I had thought I must redouble my efforts to improve myself and then, perhaps, in time, I would arrive at a lofty point of piousness capable of accepting God's love and then, bingo, I would be able to go out and achieve this great love. But where would that lead me? In my better moments, I would fall prey to the prideful belief that I could be worthy in my own right. If I could be awesome of my own accord, I would have cause for superiority over my fellow humans and be liable to judge others from my pedestal. (Spewing wrath at unsuspecting park litterers comes to mind.) Then when I inevitably failed, I would fall prey to insecurity—the other side of my over-functioning—and continue to skirt around a real relationship with God. Lacking confidence, I would play small and scared. Neither of these scenarios were the stuff of great love.

St. Thérèse helped me realize that I could already achieve this great love through dependency, not perfection. I accept God's love when I am open to allowing Him to work in me and through me. To do this, I must first recognize myself as in need of His help. This recognition is not an act of undue self-effacement, but an honest assessment of our human limitations. Then I volunteer myself as a conduit for His perfect love—the love I desire to share but cannot sustain on my own. In this way, I can shine forth even in my weakness. Yet my brilliance does not poison me against others. I understand myself and everyone else—litterers and non-litterers alike—as equally in need of God's grace, so I cannot judge. And I can better pick up trash without expectation or resentment when I consider the many graces freely given to me by God.

I paused to consider the implications of the saint's teachings: petals earn no points *and* God happily bolsters our actions with grace. Yes, the salvation on offer by Christ is a really good deal. Still, my inner skeptic was not satisfied. I had to believe our actions counted for something. A question that has bedeviled believers for time immemorial, my turn had come to contend with it. Why do our actions matter?

Ah!" answered St. Thérèse, "It is because Jesus has so incomprehensible love for us that He wills to do nothing without us. The Creator of the universe awaits the prayer of a poor little soul to save other souls redeemed like it at the price of all His Blood."[25]

Love. Love makes our actions matter. But of course! What other explanation would make sense given the circumstances? God is all powerful; He has no need of our works. God is also perfectly good; our actions cannot contribute to His goodness. Nevertheless, He created us out of love so that we might love. A product of my Catholic education, I knew we possessed free will—an ability to decide our actions—precisely so we might meaningfully love; pre-programmed automatons are incapable of heroic deeds or saintly sacrifices. Thus, our actions, however little or imperfect, indicate our desire to participate in this beautiful, radical experiment in love: making petals and litter bespoke opportunities to show the love for which we were made.

Later that week I was back at the park, picking up trash with my kids. I decided only to pick up trash to the extent it did not conflict with toodle time, but then my children, ever interested in sharing in the glory of grownup tasks, offered their assistance. Mid lesson on what constitutes trash (versus nature) and thus merits inclusion in mommy's special bag, Nicolas interrupted, "Mommy. But *why* should we make good choices?"

"*Uff*" I thought. "How should I boil that philosophical argument down to toddler speak?" Thinking it over, I responded "Well, to make the world a happier, nicer place." Nicolas beamed, adding his trash to the bag and Gabriel grinned, nary a piece of trash in or near his sweet toddler mouth.

21

SALTINE MEDITATION

I perched in my usual corner spot on our infamous red couch, well situated to watch Nicolas and Gabriel play. Today I studied them with an anthropologist's curiosity, looking for the attributes they possessed that I did not. The wisdom I had absorbed of late had sparked my interest in the topic. First, St. Thérèse, throughout her autobiography, rejoiced in her childlike state. Then I recalled Jesus' declaration: "Unless you turn and become like little children you will never enter the kingdom of heaven."[26]

Children are special; I could readily assent to that proposition. I had, after all, reached the same conclusion in my deliberations upon becoming a mother. From early on I had gravitated toward educational theories that placed their trust in a child's innate abilities. As a mother, I sought to guard this internal flame, pure and beautiful, protecting it from the wind and dangers while also exposing it to the world's oxygenating wonders. And in a million treasured moments I had witnessed the proof of what I suspected: children have an outsized capacity to explore, create, consider, focus, and achieve. Surveying my living room, I saw Nicolas, hunched over his collections of cars, fully engaged in orchestrating their latest adventure. Gabriel, his adoring apprentice, was contently playing nearby with the portion of the fleet allocated to him.

I smiled. I loved to watch my children lost in their play, where they seemed so completely at ease, so alive.

Having resolved to unlock the secrets of a child's joyful simplicity and creative contentment, I naturally applied my trademark Type A analytical nature to the matter. My trusty notebook and pen in hand, I scribbled; "What traits do my children possess that I do not?" Surveying my subjects with my anthropologist's eye, I began:

- Effortless gratitude for life's rocks, sticks, and leaves
- Readiness to demand "Mommy help me!"
- No worries
- Enjoy looking at themselves in the mirror
- Endless love to share (even after I have been impatient with them)

Sighing, I leaned back. How many of these attributes did I have, or even could hope to acquire? The world I inhabited rarely allowed for my children's carefree existence; its challenges daily proved that, while I had joined St. Thérèse in declaring, "everything is grace," I still lacked the ability to abide peaceably by this credo. Worries and insecurities too easily robbed my focus and calm, preventing me from making the choices I desired. St. Thérèse had promised "nothing but a humble and profound peace in the depths of the heart."[27] Did my occasional (frequent?) need to discharge a scream in my laundry room hideout mean I still had a long road to improvement? And then there was my still unresolved bug bear; despite pages of practicing gratitude, I couldn't say I always *felt* loved by God. My children played only inches away, yet there seemed a chasm between us.

The kitchen's kitschy tile — a kickline of pears, apples, strawberries, and grapes — merrily mocked me as I huffed deep breaths in their direction, fruitlessly trying to find focus in the mess of emotion in which I was drowning. It was a few days after my stint as a living room anthropologist, and nausea and exhaustion were unwelcome guests at my lunch shift. I was nauseous from my latest pregnancy and exhausted by the morning's sprint to the neighborhood urgent care. The sprint was the third such trip of the month because Nicolas, then Gabriel, and then Nicolas again, mysteriously exhibited writhing stomach pain upon our arrival at the park. So harried was our stroller descent that not even the air of experienced motherhood that radiated from my entourage of tiny humans could protect me from the commentary of my (literally) old friends, the street grandma vigilantes, who once again provided obvious observations: "Excuse me. Are you aware your child is screaming his bloody head off?" While the final prognoses for the boys were nothing more than two cases of blocked plumbing and one bee sting, I wore the cumulative hardship like my sagging, third-time-around maternity jeans: lacking zip and elasticity.

The sound of my children's mounting agitation morphed into a shrill static on the periphery of my consciousness. I shook my head, again trying to focus. What should we have for lunch? I did not want to eat — the nausea saw to that. Yet, I knew from experience forcing myself to eat would temporarily abate the nausea. My exact question, therefore, was "What of the limited offerings available in my kitchen would best satiate my hunger while least aggravating my nausea?" I still had little skill and no fondness for cooking.

I grabbed a packet of saltine crackers and sat on a nearby chair. Determined to turn this day around, I munched, mentally reviewing my new principles. This moment and the morning's mayhem was a gift—an endurance course in patience. Check. My faithful execution of this lunch shift represented my best contribution to the greater good. Okay. My blood sugar stabilized, I sought to recall that which I had just learned. I had just read Dr. Gregory Bottaro's *The Mindful Catholic: Finding God One Moment at a Time*. The title had popped up on the "recommended for you" section of my audiobook account, and I thought, "Why not?" I doubted someone as old school and analytical as I could excel at mindfulness, yet I did want help staying in charge of my thoughts and feelings—and not the other way around. Thus, I had been attempting to practice the author's recommended mindfulness exercises, usually with an unnamed toddler, who no longer wished to nap, bouncing on my head.

My initial foray into mindfulness confirmed I had much to learn. Dr. Bottaro described mindfulness as awareness of the present moment with acceptance and non-judgment.[28] To take an example, a mindful response to exercises I attempted would involve calmly perceiving the energetic bonks repeatedly pummeling my tired body and the faint smell of a poopy diaper. I would also be able to recognize peaceably the feeling, "ARGH! Can't mommy just have a minute to herself?!?" and the fleeting nature of my qualms about sending my dear firstborn to preschool. Alas, my actual response was not mindful. I was frazzled and cranky and then upset with myself for being frazzled and cranky.

The book reinforced my hunch that a childlike state is the ideal. Mindfulness aims to cultivate a childlike disposition toward ourselves and others because "you can't be curious and unhappy or stressed at the same time."[29] Having definitively established a childlike state as my ideal, I was grateful for Dr. Bottaro's practical technique on how to recapture some of this simplicity. I opened my book notes:

- Just because a thought or feeling happens doesn't mean it is true. Thoughts and feelings can come out of nowhere, without our creating them, and be outside of our control. What we can control is our response to those thoughts and feelings.[30]

I felt palpable relief in first learning this: thoughts and feelings in themselves are not necessarily true or wrong. This reality was so wildly sensible once articulated, yet it was not one I had deduced in all my years of feeling, over-thinking, and kicking myself for feeling and over-thinking.

It was a conclusive rebuttal to my worry of needing to conjure up warm sentiments of *feeling* loved to live a life of faith and recognition. While St. Thérèse promised, "nothing but a humble and profound peace in the depths of the heart," she also declared, "I told myself that charity must not consist in feelings but in works."[31] I felt empowered knowing what counted was not whatever mess of feelings threw up on me; rather, what mattered were the actions I took to respond to them. Opening another cracker packet, I kept reading:

- We encounter problems when we place implicit trust in the reality of our thoughts; when we do not think about how we are thinking.[32]

- Additionally, much of reality is experienced not as it really is, but as we interpret it to be through a filter. This filter is a function of the brain's autopilot learning and is created by our own experience; the habits we develop trigger thoughts, and those thoughts trigger feelings.[33]

- While the brain's autopilot function serves an important purpose, it is problematic when we use it to perceive dangers

> that either don't exist or don't exist to the degree we imagine. When this happens we tend to lose perception and inadvertently believe thoughts and feelings that aren't true.[34] Our inner critic often speaks loudest when we are stressed.[35]

This fascinating insight on the brain, combined with my new writing project, revealed to me how cynical and mean my subconscious had become: "You have to be exceptional in order to count," my Manhattan education hissed; "Only fools trust," my jungle initiation insisted; and "You are failing them," my mother guilt railed. Shortcomings, heaven knew I had them. But this filter would never build me up or believe me good enough. How to get unstuck? I read on.

- Mindfulness puts space between us and our negative thoughts and feelings, allowing us to better understand them, and, as a consequence, better make the choices we desire—those that align with our values.[36]
- When we practice mindfulness, we can see thoughts and feelings as mental events as they occur in the mind, meandering by like clouds, and we are free from the pressure to solve a problem or escape a danger.[37]
- Crucial to our ability to see our negative thoughts and feelings with acceptance and non-judgement—with a child's curiosity—is a child's sense that their world is protected and cared for and that their needs are met without them knowing how or why.[38] Adults can maintain a similar outlook when they trust God to love and care for them in every situation.[39]

Okay. The solution to my lunch shift was clear. I needed a first course of mindfulness. I best understood the "how" of practicing mindfulness as an augmented gratitude practice. Seeking mindfulness, I would prayerfully, slowly name all phenomena I was aware of in any given moment. If "everything is grace," I reasoned, this exercise helped me see the gifts I had been given. Once aware of my mental and physical landscape, I could best decide what to do. I might see the need to exert my will to override base intentions, call out my subconscious for being a meanie pants liar, or tell myself it is okay to feel this way.

I had developed another possible tactic based on the combined advice of Dr. Bottaro and my favorite Christian author C.S. Lewis. Dr. Bottaro explained that thinking your way out of certain situations is akin to a computer trying to open another program to solve the problem of too many programs being open. He recommended in such situations we should not engage these thoughts and or try to argue our way out of them. Instead, we should simply close tabs down.[40] At first, I considered this advice downright revolutionary. I did, after all, love to analyze. Then I remembered one of my favorite C.S. Lewis quotes: God wants us to think of the future "just so much as is necessary for now planning the acts of justice or charity which will probably be their duty tomorrow."[41] If I were honest with myself, my thinking was often actually worrying. Now that I had seen worrying for what it was—counterproductive to a true relationship with God and an enormous waste of time and energy—I was eager to swear it off. So I created a brief questionnaire to identify when I might need to stop thinking:

Can I do anything about what I am concerned about?

Yes, then do it.

No, then close tabs down.

I felt my nausea fade as the bland carbohydrates had their desired effect. I closed my notebook and began my mindfulness practice. What was I mindful of now? Well there was an "I'm pregnant" pity party, subconsciously sabotaging my motivation with thoughts of "My life is unfairly hard" and "I can't believe I had to make *three* trips to urgent care this month. *This month!*" Then there was a heap of uncomfortable vulnerability with three lives dependent on me to resolve their hunger, blocked plumbing, and so much more. And, of course, the physical strain of pregnancy. All combined, a perfect recipe for missing the comfort and support of family and friends far away, my weakest point. I winced in recognition of these lurking emotional booby traps. Yet, even as I was adrift in dark hurt, I felt with new confidence in God's love for me. With more trust that I ever had before, I whispered Dr. Bottaro's recommended emergency prayer; "Ever present Lord here with me now. Help me be here with you."[42]

I closed my eyes and made an act of mental acceptance: "I accept my loneliness. I accept my feelings as they are, neither good nor bad. And I will not—should not—beat myself up for having them." Opening my eyes, I turned to naming the aspects of my environment: that blasted fruit motif, saltine crackers and their revitalizing properties, sounds of my mischievous duo, the excitement of new life, and rice and beans at the ready.

I took a deep breath, stood up, and went back to preparing lunch—the usual chicken, rice, beans, veggie combo that I could have known all along would be our fare, had I been thinking mindfully. I recalled another of Dr. Bottaro's assertions: God desires us to be at our most productive, and we are most productive in a childlike state.[43] Our creativity and perceptive thinking work best when we are not frantic and stressed.[44]

God's caring about a concept as seemingly crass as productivity at first amused me. I imagined the archetypical white-bearded man in the sky poring over bar charts and key performance indicators. Then, I was strangely pleased. I felt affirmed knowing my love of productivity was not some twitchy character defect, but a positive attribute. I was also delighted to learn that a state of maximum productivity was not characteristically miserable. I could easily believe that the output of a child's carefree existence trumped the output of, say, a drab, windowless conference room. I only had to consider the staggering accomplishments ratcheted up by my own children in their first years of life: immobility to literal leaps and bounds, illiteracy to bilingual fluency, and their own effervescent creativity. Nicolas graduated from my Highchair Confinement Program when he created a semi-truck from the Cheerios and banana peel left on his tray.

When lunch was ready, I sat with my boys, greeting them and my newest opportunity to love and be loved.

22

LEAN IN

Having just awakened from another night of insufficient sleep, I lay in bed wondering how I would ever meet the demands of the day.

A week earlier, I had been horrified to discover upon using the bathroom that I was bleeding. Just shy of 10 weeks pregnant, dread instantly sank its pernicious claws into me. I placed a frantic call to Josh. He had just informed his board of directors that his co-founder Benedikt, the tenacious "never quit" German, had decided to leave. His departure, besides leaving Josh to carry the executive load alone, was liable to indicate a vote of no confidence in the business.

"What do you want me to do?" he asked. His response rang with his characteristic action-oriented problem solving, a hallmark of what males consider compassion and the bane of their female counterparts everywhere. The unspoken current was the many fires he had to put out before his day was through. I sighed. I did not know what to do. I had been unable to reach my obstetrician and my doctor cousin told me a miscarriage was unlikely since the baby had a heartbeat at the seven-week ultrasound. Josh and I exchanged a few more attempts at comfort, and I hung up just as Nicolas began a meltdown, the result of his earlier refusal to take a nap. I needed a plan and fast. Wiping my tears to avoid aggravating the situation with a "let's all mirror mama's mood" death spiral, I was saved by a flash of insight. I could do an ultrasound at the neighborhood clinic. My recent sprints had prepared me for this moment. I knew they had a machine on site because a doctor had scanned Nicolas' abdomen. I immediately called Josh back, and he promised to come home after his next call. I greeted him soon after with a hug and a sob and then left for urgent care.

I could not stop crying, even in the company of strangers awaiting triage. A kind nurse moved me to a private room to wait. I tried to take deep breaths to still my tears and prayed the mindfulness emergency prayer—"Ever present Lord here with me now. Help me be here with you"—in almost maniacal repetition. I then decided to switch to a rosary and began by recalling the mystery assigned to that particular day of the week. Tuesday called for the Sorrowful Mysteries. My heart sank.

Another nurse arrived to take me for my ultrasound. Lying on the table, I focused my attention on a solitary ceiling light feebly illuminating my sterile surroundings. A doctor arrived and began her examination. Eternal minutes passed. I listened for words of comfort, but there was only silence. Finally, I summoned the courage to ask, "What do you observe?" She started, saying, "It is smaller than expected. It looks only seven weeks developed." And then she reluctantly finished, "I can't find a heartbeat." Breaking out again into sobs, I placed my hand over my eyes, blocking out the light, along with the doctor's bland assurances that it was nothing I did or did not do and the nurse's eager attempts to offer me a glass of water.

Josh met me at the door with another hug. Nicolas' questioning eyes showed us he would have to be told. Crouching down to meet his gaze, I said, "The baby is done growing in mommy's tummy. The baby is in heaven." Josh then scooped him up in his lap and said gently, "The baby died. Do you know what that means?" He did not respond and soon squirmed away, but I knew with a mother's confidence that he had heard.

Two days later, I again had to answer Nicolas' questioning eyes, this time hoping they did not notice the fear in my own. Upon leaving urgent care I had been instructed to expect anything, ranging from a drastic, spontaneous increase in bleeding requiring immediate medical attention or, perhaps, nothing at all. Unable to finance full coverage childcare for possible symptoms at an undetermined time, I had been on my own with the kids all day. When the afternoon brought increased bleeding and the sensation of early labor, I placed another frantic call to Josh, telling him to come home immediately. I strained to maintain an air of calm while waiting for him to arrive. "Mommy doesn't feel good right now. Can you go play nicely in the living room?" I pleaded, silently praying for a docile acceptance of my request. Shortly after, Josh arrived along with Benedikt and his girlfriend, departing comrades providing a final assist as last-minute babysitting recruits.

Hours later I was again inconsolable in Josh's arms in the familiar lobby of the maternity hospital, the statue of the Blessed Mother loyally standing watch. I had completed all the necessary procedures and was free to leave. Yet I could not bring myself to cross the hospital's turnstile threshold. I viscerally balked at leaving what was left of my baby—bled out in indistinct blobs here and there—with no opportunity to give him or her a dignified end. But what recourse did I have? I had no body to bury, no ceremony to provide comfort, no knowledge of the sex to even give a name. I was powerless. Finally, when a security guard offered to escort me to a private room, I allowed Josh to lead me out. Before exiting, I glanced back at the statue and beseeched my familiar friend, the Blessed Mother, "You will take care of my baby, right?"

I remained tired, so tired. I had been tired for weeks. Not too long ago I had joked it was because I was growing arms and legs, but the new reality was it derived from a life decomposing inside of me. I sighed and asked again to no one in particular, a version of the question I asked myself when I first woke. "How do I survive the day?"

I sat at the neighborhood coffee shop, anxiously tapping my pen against the table. I had wandered there not long before. Following my miscarriage, Josh found he could best care for me by ushering me out the door with a confident "I got this." Extracted from my rabbit hole of childcare and household responsibilities, I had no choice but to face the tumult within me. Released to the sidewalks of São Paulo, an internal angst drove me to walk and wander, wander and walk, seemingly searching for a baby my head knew was gone but my body did not. While my recent lessons allowed for a faithful acceptance of this "everything is grace" moment, I struggled to cope with exhaustion and haywire hormones.

This day, however, I sat and opened my notebook. I stared at the blank page before me as if to demand of it, "What am I searching for if not my baby?" I reluctantly acknowledged the question that had been smoldering beneath the petal-strewing treadmill on which I had been sprinting. I slowly wrote: "How can I love without running out of love?" I had no answer. "Self-care! Me-time! Boundaries!" I had been told. While I valued such practices, I found them either insufficient or impossible during my life's hardest stretches. I feared the question might be not *how* but *if* we can love without running out. I wondered, "Was I doomed to break? Would I eventually find myself just too tired to rise yet again and meet the day's demands?" Perhaps I could survive this crisis marathon, but what about another?

There would be another, I was sure. What if, by completing the race of my golden mothering days, I would cross the finish line washed up and spent, with nothing left to give?

Two days later I strode out of our apartment complex bound for the coffee shop, eager to digest my latest epiphanies. Since I last visited I had been struck by two lightning bolts so precisely responding to my anxieties that I could not doubt they were lobbed down from on high just for me.

The first was a homily by Bishop Barron in which he reflects on the Old Testament tale of a widow who was preparing to fix a last meal for herself and her son, after which they would likely perish, victims of their poverty and a combined drought and famine.[45] When the prophet Elijah comes to their door, he audaciously asks her for a cup of water. She protests, citing her desperate circumstances. Elijah ups the ante, asking her to bring him a cake, as well. As Bishop Barron noted, it would be funny if it weren't so tragic. The woman ultimately decides to give Elijah what he asks for, only to find that her jar of flour did not run empty nor her jug of oil run dry, illuminating a Biblical paradox: abundance comes from the willing gift.[46] Precisely when we are at our most vulnerable—when our instinct is to hoard our precious remaining resources or call it quits—God asks us to give. When we are linked to the God who is nothing but giving we can give and give and never run out.

The second came from a book recommended by my high school friends: *I Believe in Love: A Personal Retreat Based on the Teachings of St. Thérèse of Lisieux* by Fr. Jean C.J. D'Eblée. Imbued by the ethos of my petal guide, Fr. D'Eblée declares, "The Cross, taken up hesitantly, is crushing; taken smilingly, by free will, and with love, it will carry you much more than you carry it."[47]

My notebook again opened to the near-empty page, I contemplated how to best summarize the answer to my question I had discovered. I confidently wrote, "Lean in!" I had to laugh. Who would have guessed? The mantra of my generation's female overachievers was the answer after all. Just not in the way we thought. Leaning into our careers and achievement does not help us nearly as much as leaning into our crosses and God's grace.

It was early on a Monday, and I had hit the kitchen with force. As usual, I had much to do before I ran out of steam. I darted about, simultaneously preparing breakfast and a crockpot dinner, all while loudly singing along to the soundtrack of my alma mater's liturgical choir. I was lost in my work and a lively Irish hymn—almost shouting the refrain "Listen to your people calling!"—when I felt an invisible embrace and a wave of peaceful assurance.

The feeling passed as quickly as it came. I stopped, amazed. Throughout the emotional tumult of my miscarriage I had consoled myself with my mindfulness education, that it was okay to feel as I did and that God loved me even when I did not feel it. Reminding myself that what mattered was an act of the will, I had battled to maintain a charitable equilibrium despite the circumstances. And then, so very unexpectedly, this brush with the divine punctuated the darkness in which I was soldiering, tenderly inviting me onward and to healing.

23

MISSION

Josh and I stood on the far side of the Colorado River, admiring the Austin skyline at sunset. Weeks before, our parents had banded together to whisk the kids and me away to Texas so I might regain my strength in the kindness and hospitality of my in-laws. Later, when Josh joined us Stateside, he and I escaped to Austin to enjoy a pleasure nearly extinct in our lives: the diaper-free weekend. Also unencumbered by pregnancy or nursing—an equally rare occurrence—I was free to let my messy mom hair down and…scoot. Unfortunately, scootering, a mode of transportation appropriately popular in the Texas capital of weird, came as natural to me as it did to one of the local armadillos attempting the same feat.

"Remind me how this is supposed to be fun?!" I yelled at Josh as he—empowered by his yee-haw native Texan aptitude—zipped far ahead of me. Beholden to a mother's cautious sensibilities, no matter my hair, I saw the sidewalk between us not as adventure, but as a giant armadillo collision course. I had all but given up on the day's "fun," resigned to trudging alongside my scooter, until we arrived at the city's Zilker Park. There I encountered manicured trails, flanked by generous, grassy medians, enabling even a scaredy cat amateur like me to feign scooting proficiency. Finally keeping pace with my husband, I relished the crisp December air, the exhilaration of rapid movement, and the ever-changing reel of high-quality people-watching.

The trail's end perfectly coincided with dusk and a river-framed cityscape. We paused to take it in. Peering out at the urban expanse, the question—"Would we ever like to live here?"—breezily floated by. A thriving, cool city within driving distance from the charming, country home of Josh's deep Texas roots; in the abstract world of *someday,* it seemed pretty ideal. The carefree twilight beckoning contemplation, another question drifted through: how would I engage with such a world? It was a question that involved both my strongest ambition, the desire to faithfully live out my highest and best use, and my darkest wound, loneliness. This question could have easily cast angst on the evening's hypothetical dreaming. Instead, it brought only a fleeting crop of pleasant what-ifs. I possessed the happy calm of having discovered a simple practice encompassing all I had learned about achieving my highest and best use. We follow God's will through fidelity to our duties appointed by Him in the present moment.

Brilliant in its simplicity, this practice is equally simple in its application. Jean-Pierre de Caussade, an 18th century French priest whose spiritual classic *Abandonment to Divine Providence* discusses this practice, asserts we can achieve holiness by faithfully performing our assigned duties "just as medicine taken obediently will produce health even though the sick person neither knows nor wishes to know anything about the medicine."[48] Thus, we can achieve our highest and best uses without fancy spiritual programs or advanced knowledge. We must only submit to all of our duties, even those we do not like or understand. It was in accepting a visiting angel's bizarre request that she "conceive and give birth to a son" that Mary enabled the salvation of humanity.[49]

In this state of abandonment, we obey God in all our duties while boldly believing that His unconditional love will remedy our limitations. If we lean solely on the performance of our duties and avoid the need for a heavenly assist, we inevitably meet our limitations and despair. On the other hand, we risk presumption, or taking God's mercy for granted, when we maintain a bold confidence in God but do not sincerely try to follow His will. While petals are not points and God happily works with our best efforts, God does want our best efforts. Our journey toward holiness must be conscious, sustained, and diligent. Obedience to and bold confidence in God; therein lies our path to perfection.

How are we to recognize our all-important duties? Fr. Caussade defines duties as either "obeying laws of God and the Church and fulfilling all duties imposed upon us by our way of life" or to "lovingly accept all God sends us at each moment of the day."[50]

While the duties (*ahem* petals) imposed by my way of life were obvious and abundant—usually identifiable by a shrill "Mommy!" or an onslaught of basic needs requiring my attention—I gained confidence in my ability to discern my duties only after I returned "do" to its proper place. When I saw duties as necessary to earn salvation, I felt a constant, frantic pressure to accomplish. I was too often the proverbial Martha, the Gospel figure best known for being "anxious and worried about many things," overwhelmed, and fuming at those who dare idle.[51]

Through my laundry room leveling I came to see the wisdom of Martha's sister Mary's approach, with most of my *aha* moments occurring in quiet contemplation. When I developed a healthier relationship with my actions, I became more capable of the calm receptivity necessary for the discernment of God's will. While abandonment requires us to accept categorically our duties, it is not fatalism. We must proactively discern God's will so it—rather than the "many things"—guides our actions. Angelic messengers with explicit requests being rare, good discernment far more often involves a combination of sitting at the feet of the Lord and our best judgment.

In my own discernment, I learned to monitor when my habitual bustle no longer served its intended beneficiary. While I'll never wax poetic about the bliss I experienced in, say, leaving the dirty dishes, I became more at ease sitting at the feet of others. I also began to recognize the baby unexpectedly awake or a toddler meltdown not as inopportune annoyances, but as sacred duties, divinely curated just for me. And, I regularly reminded myself, the duty to "loving acceptance of all God sends us at each moment" includes joys as well as sorrows; "toodling" with my children was just as much my sacred duty as making them lunch.

Adopting this approach to my highest and best use, I found myself with an unexpected output: creativity. I had long harbored an inkling that I should create but could never determine a medium. Or, more accurately, I never gave myself permission or the time. Better to stay within the safety and objectivity of accountancy and Excel spreadsheets. In learning to embrace vulnerability, I could accept the messiness of the creative process. When pestered by insecurities, I fell back on a stubborn obedience to the command I received: "Write!"

During my Texas repose I continued to write in the afternoon lull, my boys having tired themselves out with the rocks, sticks, and leaves of Texas. I took solace in the story that slowly emerged from a collection of disparate text. As I had gleaned from that park bench sob, I would always be lonely if I were not brave enough to show others the parts of myself I believed to be weak, quirky, or unlikeable. So in taking this chance, baring my hurts and graces, I hoped it would lead me to fellowship and trusted that my experience would be of use to someone with similar struggles. How exactly I did not know. But I did not need to know. Because I was happy to get there one step, one duty, one day at a time. And my duty in that moment was as simple as scooting with my husband into a western sunset.

24

YEAR SEVEN

Our seven-year anniversary in Brazil loomed.

Blissfully unaware that our mountain top, ocean view engagement constituted a mystical pact to relocate and begin a life in Brazil, we had been equally unaware that, following seven trips around the sun in the sunny tropics, we would still be there struggling. Seven years. The outer range of the time by which we assumed we would be safely back in the States, rolling in financial flexibility. Magnifying the gravitas of this anniversary, it fell just two days before my latest pregnancy's due date. The cosmic pressure of these twin dates demanded, "Have you figured out your life yet?"

I had been nervous about leaving my Texas repose, wondering if the return to Brazil would again level me. I had, as I set out, definitively reevaluated the way I understood the world. But my newfound wisdom had not yet faced the tests of pressure, normalcy, and time. Thankfully, I hurdled the challenges of reentry in stride, entering the laundry room only for the purposes of washing clothes. Resuming my everyday life, I keenly felt the difficulties of caring for two kids while pregnant, aka trying not to pee my pants in public and cursing the number of times life required me to bend over. Expecting a fast labor, I nervously joked with my neighborhood acquaintances: "My only goal is to make it to hospital in time" and "I can leave these boys with you if needed, right?" Yet, again, none of these hardships had rendered me a puddle. I hoped that maybe, just maybe, I had life figured out.

And then, I said "no" to the rodeo. The largest rodeo in Latin America. Josh had fancied going for years, but canceled our booking when I melted down at the prospect of packing for yet another trip only to leave home's assured access to a bathroom near a comfortable chair.

The day we would have been at the rodeo, I sat, where else, but our miserable red couch, beating myself up on the misery of the day. Josh and I both had been in a slump lately. He was exhausted from years of a perpetual fight to stave off bankruptcy and I from my continued isolation. Cooped up in our dismal apartment rather than pleasantly distracted, tensions boiled over into shouts, the details of which were not especially important. Every couple has their script. After sending Josh out the door yelling, I turned to face two bright faces. Wiping a tear, I huffed to the couch to compose myself and collect my thoughts.

While enlightened to the fallacy that I must earn love through my actions (say, agreeing to the rodeo), I still felt insecure for having disappointed my family by acknowledging my limits. Having only recently awakened to the perils of equating my worth with my actions, my wounds were far from healed. I wore them like hidden fault lines. Josh had been understanding when canceling, yet a performance evaluation, real or imagined, could still cause me pain. Then there was the ugliness of the morning. In its wake, all that I wanted to be for my family, a source of light and inspiration, seemed a load of hooey. Slumping into the couch, guilt mocked my hope that I had graduated from my journey a new and improved human being. That I had it "figured out."

My children jumped up on me, and I stole hugs of comfort, breathing in their mischievous smiles and wriggly frames so precious to me I could explode. As my arms wrapped around them, raw vulnerability and thanksgiving engulfed me in a cloud. I wanted life to be perfect for them, and I wanted to be perfect for them. Yet my expanded mother's heart and 33 years knew that neither today, tomorrow, nor a someday future would hold perfection for them, or for me. At least in the way I had understood it. That "other side" I used to count on in my prayers, the one I just had to believe was possible to reach with enough hard work and gumption, did not exist. I knew that now. How then could I bear this weight? My sorrows, my faults, and all that could go wrong.

My children scampered off, and a lifetime of habit shrilly insisted that I sweep away all my failed attempts and once more set out to create a world without problems, a home where no one shouts, and a mother with no hidden sadness. I did not want to enact the discipline necessary to entrust my pathetic best efforts to God. I did not want God or anyone else to see this mess. "WHAT'S THE POINT?" I wanted to scream. Instead, I inhaled deeply and then gently, firmly reminded myself of what I had learned: I had an answer for suffering and human weakness.

I believed in a Savior who willingly faced every horror imaginable, only to emerge triumphant. Jesus saved us through His passion, death and resurrection; I had known this since youth but had not always experienced its comfort. When I mistakenly believed I had to earn God's love, His gruesome, voluntary death weighed on me like an enormously uncomfortable debt that was best kept at the periphery of my consciousness until I could hurry up and pay it back. The insecure overachiever in me wondered: if Jesus suffered so we might be saved, should I, too, desire greater suffering to promote greater glory? Lacking a firm answer, my subconscious was left to reason, "I could settle my debt faster if my lot were harder," perversely causing me to wish suffering upon myself.

In coming to understand God's love as merciful, I also came to understand suffering anew, endeavoring to live as St. Thérèse professed, "Neither do I desire any longer suffering or death, and still I love them both; it is *love* alone that attracts me…Now, abandonment alone guides me. I have no other compass!"[52] A rather strange, shocking declaration: to "love" suffering. Yet, St. Thérèse knew love cannot exist without sacrifice and that God is always working for our good. Thus, when suffering arose, she welcomed it as an inevitable traveling companion for a life rooted in love.

Emerging from my journey better able to accept suffering and the God's gift of salvation, I was able to see the cross as an act as lovely as it was awful. What loveliness did I see? That I was never alone in my pain and that my sins could not scare Him. Such was the intensity of anguish Jesus endured on the cross that He cried out "My God, My God, why have you forsaken me?" His own, "WHAT'S THE POINT?" Reflecting upon Jesus' dying words, theologian G.K Chesterton argued, "God seemed for an instant to be an atheist."[53] Jesus then went on to spend three days in the depth of hell where He continued to experience the worst of human behavior and misery. No sin or suffering exists that Jesus did not face. Of my own pain, He felt the ache of loneliness when His closest friends abandoned or betrayed Him on the eve of His execution.

No, God is not afraid of our darkness. God does his best work in the dark. The cross is His enduring proof that in the fullness of time the wreckage of the world will be made right — the long awaited perfect. Through the cross Jesus assumed all sin and suffering only to transform it into the triumph of the resurrection. In understanding the cross as a means to a glorious end, we can join Saint John Paul II in proclaiming, "Do not abandon yourselves to despair. We are the Easter people and hallelujah is our song."[54] The day irreparably a disaster, I could not imagine life without this comfort.

Closing my eyes, I once again committed to achieving my highest and best use: a path of falling and getting back up until kingdom come.

I crawled into bed next to Josh, bringing the long, icky day to a close. After seven years of indefatigable effort and dashed hopes, we knew well this type of goodnight: side by side in sadness yet helpless to ease the hurt of the other.

My turn to lead prayer, I said simply, "Pick up our broken pieces. Draw straight with our crooked lines. Fix what we have left undone." and closed with the sign of the cross, an easily overlooked reminder of the life we commit to when choosing to walk with Christ.

I rolled over, glancing at the well-thumbed stack of books on my nearby shelf, the saints and souls that guided my journey, standing watch still. Heartened by this mystical fellowship, I closed my eyes to memories from the day. I saw again the bright faces of my children, my constant reminders of the wonder and creativity possible with faithful simplicity. Placing my hands on the babe to come, I slept in the assurance that I can accomplish great deeds in He who strengthens me.

25

ANNIVERSARY PRESENT

Legs akimbo on either side of my belly, I rested serenely on a salon chair. Having just finished a manicure and pedicure (a most enjoyable way to pass the eternal hours that comprise any day past one's due date), I lingered to let the polish set. I still hoped to avoid a C-section birth, yet I did not see this as preventing me from participating in the other local birth custom: beauty hour! Given that the human body completely replaces its cells over a seven-year period, I partook in this pre-labor ritual fully Brazilian. The finishing spray on my makeover: I had a blowout scheduled for that afternoon. I was to report to the hospital the next morning for an induction that would entice my baby into the world and wanted to look my best.

The pampering also served as a celebration of trials survived. As if a final test before granting me full Brazilian status, my jungle home had prepared a "greatest hits" round of challenges. It kicked things off with the prerequisite baseline tension of a do-or-die investment round circling ever closer to my due date. Then it tossed in a cracked pipe that rendered my kitchen sink inoperable, which coincided with a weekend of solo parenting during which I also had to take Nicolas to urgent care for a mystery ailment. For the grand finale, it masterfully combined a *jeitinho* solution with an insect plague. The landlord resolved the issue of my kitchen sink by drilling a child-sized hole in the wall, liberating the cockroaches I had been battling.

Dancing with each of these trials, I leaned on a tune of my own. In quiet moments I put in my earbuds, closed my eyes and allowed the Beatles' "Let It Be" to envelop me in solace and grace:

> *When I find myself in times of trouble*
> *Mother Mary comes to me speaking words of wisdom,*
> *let it be*
> *And in my hour of darkness she is standing*
> *right in front of me*
> *Speaking words of wisdom, let it be*
> *Let it be, let it be*
> *Let it be, let it be*
> *Whisper words of wisdom*
> *Let it be*

Picking up on my third trimester anthem, Nicolas began to sing, "Let it pee, let it pee! Let it pee, let it pee!" An interpretation as humorous as it was logical; he knew me to be either in the bathroom or at a doctor's appointment whenever I was not beached somewhere in sight.

Taking advantage of this beauty hour repose, I quietly hummed my song, inviting strength for the uncertainties of the coming day. I had given no thought to an induction; I had been confident that I would have a fast, normal labor. Yet my due date and my sister's visit had passed, the clock had started on my parents' visit, and my doctor had made a persuasive case for its merits.

Rising from my chair polished and calm, I waddled down to the park to meet my mom and the boys. Arriving, I sat again, soaking up the sun ahead of my stay in the hospital fortress and enjoying the company of the Millennial Club; "My, don't you look well. Are you sure you wouldn't be more comfortable at home, say knitting?"

Soon after back home (not to knit, but to prepare lunch) I felt a cramp that, while not particularly painful, I intuitively knew to be an opening salvo. I had been feeling odd pains for weeks. Those I experienced the weekend before my sister's arrival turned me into a bundle of nerves, so sure was I that destiny would see me tossing an iPad babysitter in my hospital bag for the boys. But now the true, peaceful voice of my honed maternal instinct whispered, "It's go time." Springing methodically into action, I called my doctor, ate a plate of rice and bean goodness, and showered. Josh arrived home and we kissed the boys, Gabriel half napping and Nicolas determined to be brave for a moment he knew to be important.

Josh focused on the road while I white-knuckled the car's overhead handle and battled a cacophony of annoyances; contractions, red lights, potholes, and (bonus!) daytime traffic typical of a city of 12 million people. When a flatbed truck backed out in front of us, paralyzing traffic, my first thought was "I must remember to tell Nicolas and Gabriel about that."

Entering the lobby, I greeted the familiar statue of Mary and the many emotions evoked by this place, grateful that the day before, a quiet wait for routine tests had allowed me to sit with the memory of the baby I lost.

Approaching triage, I looked forward to VIP treatment. Now savvy to secrets disclosed to those fully Brazilian, I had found a doctor I liked and was covered by our insurance plan. For the first time, a familiar face would oversee my labor! Moreover, this doctor informed me that I could request to complete the hospital check-in procedures from a private room made available to multiparous mothers at risk of scaring innocent bystanders with a waiting room delivery. Normal births are known to get successively faster. No more waiting on an impersonal, all-powerful monitor!

I relayed my request to the triage nurse as advised and was delighted to receive an immediate medical examination. A dilation ruling of six centimeters substantiated my claims to preferred access. I again inquired about the private room. The doctor and nurse nodded acquiescently and commenced with their ritual preparatory activity, including hijacking Josh for scrub in and trading my clothes for a hospital gown.

The nurse then led me down the hall, and I imagined what comforts awaited me. A private doula? My own bucket of ice chips? Egyptian cotton hospital gowns with matching slippers? Opening this velvet rope of hospital doors she revealed…the same holding pen for pregnant women I had been in the day before for my routine tests. A dozen eyes turned in unison to look at me and I suddenly felt very aware of the limited coverage of my actual gown.

A new nurse nonchalantly directed me to an available chair for an echocardiogram test, a procedure I knew to be routine *before* labor and required 20-odd minutes sitting still. I gave her a pained "you've got to be kidding me" look, and she quickly folded. She left me to consult with another nurse, the commanding, clipboard queen bee of this pregnant women holding pen, and returned with new instructions. I needed a slow drip of fluids. Getting nowhere with my pleas to see my doctor or my husband, I grudgingly acquiesced to the procedure.

I paced and huffed in the radius allowed by my IV stand, my fellow inmates in this farcical VIP lounge now straining to feign polite obliviousness of my blustering presence. With their own deliveries approaching they would have surely preferred I were left to scare the general population of the waiting room rather than provide them with this closeup preview of active labor.

I focused on my breathing and the progress of my slow drip, then remembered my intention to offer up my pain for women struggling to accept their worth. Following an eternity of my best patience, the clipboard queen informed me that I was cleared for admittance. Gurney cruising, delivery room bound, a jubilant "…and we are off!" resounded through my pain; the long wait was almost over. Josh and my delivery dream team met me in the corridor of the birthing wing and we greeted each other with the conviviality of the start of a great party.

"There is a Black Friday special on babies, so we have to wait here until a room frees up," began Dr. Ana.

"Oh! Is that so?" I grimace-grinned in reply.

"I finally met your husband!" she continued, pointing at Josh.

A multiparous dad, Josh had not accompanied me to the doctor since, oh, about a thousand appointments back. He smiled good-naturedly, radiating an air of surgical cleanliness following his time in hospital hostage.

Dr. Ana glowed. "And let me introduce you to Dr. Leo, the anesthesiologist. His work is the best. I would know; he did my own labor."

Quietly accepting Dr. Ana's praise, Dr. Leo began to speak but I only heard "reassuring words bla blah blah I am required to relay this information to you before I administer your epidural blah blah blah."

Interrupting him with a huff-grimace-smile sequence, I sputtered, "Great…can we start?" I never had an anesthesiologist waiting on me before!

"Here? No no…not in the hallway," he replied. Sensing my request either offended his propriety or should have offended mine, I shrugged and returned my focus to my breathing, dimly aware of talk of Black Friday deals won and lost.

A room soon came available and Dr. Leo's marvelous medication evaporated my pain into the sweet mist of the past. Placing her hands on my stomach, Dr. Ana declared it to be *bombando or* pumping. I laughed because I had only ever heard this verb used to describe club music. She then invited me to take my place on a birthing stool, and we all relocated around the blue tarp on which it sat. Looking around at the merry faces from my floor perch—my attending doctor sitting crossed-legged in front me—the mood felt as much spring picnic as it did labor and delivery end game.

Instructed to push, I felt the movement of the baby yet none of the pain. (Dr. Leo really was the man!) In a sitting position, I was able to witness this wondrous, primordial process of which I was the host. Cries soon announced the baby's arrival, and they gave her to me bloody, purple, and fresh. I held her tight against my chest for that most magical of moments: meeting a new love. Reluctantly giving her back for necessary medical checks, I glanced up at the clock and laughed. The hour just before 5:00, a salon chair sat empty and a blow dryer idle. Tucking a wisp of frizzy hair behind my ear, I returned to staring happily at my baby, beautiful and calm.

The door opened and Nicolas and Gabriel burst into our hospital room. "Where's Sis?" Gabriel exclaimed as they both beelined past my outstretched arms. Finding her in the bassinet, Gabriel crawled up onto my lap and Nicolas onto Josh's to see better. Gabriel reached out to touch her, and Nicolas swatted his hand away, proudly declaring, "Hi! I'm Nico."

My mother's heart brimmed watching this dance of siblings newly established; doting and protective, enthusiastic and shy. I smiled, recalling the recent moment when this scene was foreshadowed. I had just emerged from the park bathroom giddy with emotion after having seen two pink lines appear on a pregnancy test, only to happen upon three ducklings, impossibly adorable, waddling united toward me.

"Do you know the baby's name?" Josh asked the boys. Responding with the characteristic determination, Gabriel announced, "Teresa. Her name is Teresa."

26

DEAR DAUGHTER

My dear daughter, Teresa.

You have your father's piercing blue eyes and lashes so long they arch back hitting your lids. Every day you muster new sounds and expressions, so anxious are you to engage with the world. I especially love holding you when I'm worn down by a particularly difficult go. I like to rub my nose against your soft cheeks and take in your innocent sweetness. In these moments I rock you gently, hoping to give you enough love and strength to last your lifetime. This life can be hard, and we women are more often entrusted with the hidden, humble petals on which greatness unfolds only in the long expanse of time.

While pregnant with you I read that mothers are usually idealized or vilified, but rarely viewed objectively. So I say to you: this is me. I told my story as truthfully as my own perspective allows. I wrote much of it with you within or resting upon me. Judge me kindly. I hurt and I am healing. I am "sorrowful, but always rejoicing."[55] And I am doing my best. Sometimes in a task master, drill sergeant, overfunctioning kind of way, I know.

You, my child, will always be perfect to me. Tis' my right as your mother. Your bubbly personality and bewitching eyes transform even the most mundane moments of our little life into magic. Still, I know as a daughter of Eve as well as of mine, insecurity is a demon you will face. Wave upon sinister wave will whisper lies of your unworthiness and a time will come when you'll meet my googly eyes of admiration with an exasperated sigh.

When these seeds of doubt take root, I implore you to fight. Fight to believe God loves you unconditionally and upon this and only this your worth depends. Fight to believe you are not your actions, appearance, feelings, relationships, or mistakes. You are you. And you are loved. Fight to believe that God loves you perfectly unlike any love you've ever known, with eyes far googlier than mine.

And beware: the crossfire is most intense when you tread on the sacred ground of your life's mission. Never have I written without a voice hissing, "boring!" Nor may I ever be free of the terror of an inadequate response to "So, what do you do?" Now mother to three, I daily face my own limitations and daily I set a new record for consecutive bad hair days. Yet, I feel alive, so alive. And this, my dearest daughter, is my deepest wish for you, that you, too, find the glorious, jubilant love for which you were made.

Love, Mom

POSTSCRIPT

Josh and I moved to Brazil accompanied only by four suitcases and our dreams in 2012. We returned to the United States with fourteen suitcases and our three Brazilian-born children in 2020. Josh's startup was a casualty of COVID. I will forever be grateful for my Brazil experience and for the wisdom it bequeathed.

RESOURCES

3. *BEM VINDO*

1. "*Portuguese for the Perplexed.*" The Economist, May 24, 2013.

5. MASTER'S IN *MERDA*

2. The World Health Organization, *The World Health Report.* 2000.

6. DISILLUSION

3. "*Petrobras reduz ativos em R$51 bil.*" Valor Econômico, April 23, 2015, p. 1.

11. CONTINUING EDUCATION

4. Cain Miller, Caitlin. *"The Costs of Motherhood are Rising and Catching Women Off Guard."* The New York Times. August 17, 2018.

13. RETREAT

5. Yakob, Laith. "*Zika Virus after the Public Health Emergency of International Concern, Brazil.*" Center for Disease Control. April 2022.

18. BATTLE LINES

6. Fiudo, Maureen. "Resigned or Consenting?" Blessed Is She. August 20, 2018.

19. PETALS AND *MERDA*

7. St. Thérèse of Lisieux, *Her Last Conversations*, ICS Publications, 1977.
8. St. Thérèse of Lisieux, *The Story of a Soul*, Double Day, 2001, p.2.
9. St. Thérèse of Lisieux, *The Story of a Soul*, Double Day, 2001, p.196.
10. Catechism of the Catholic Church, USCB Publishing, 1995, Paragraph 1996.
11. Philippians 4:6-7
12. Voskamp, Ann. *One Thousand Gifts*, Zondervan, 2011, p.148.
13. St. Catherine of Siena

20. LESSONS IN LITTER

14. Barron, Robert. "*Summed Up in Christ.*" Word on Fire. July 15, 2018.

15. Ephesians 1:4

16. St. Thérèse of Lisieux, *The Story of a Soul,* Double Day, 2001, p.192.

17. St. Thérèse of Lisieux, *The Story of a Soul,* Double Day, 2001, p.192.

18. 1 Corinthians 12:29

19. 1 Corinthians 13:4-7

20. St. Thérèse of Lisieux, *The Story of a Soul,* Double Day, 2001, p.194.

21. St. Thérèse of Lisieux, *The Story of a Soul,* Double Day, 2001, p.195.

22. St. Thérèse of Lisieux, *The Story of a Soul,* Double Day, 2001, p.165, 187, 189, 196, and 200.

23. St. Thérèse of Lisieux, *The Story of a Soul,* Double Day, 2001, p.195.

24. St. Thérèse of Lisieux, *The Story of a Soul,* Double Day, 2001, p.197.

25. LT 135 From Thérèse to Céline. Les archives du Carmel de Lisieux. August 15, 1982.

21. SALTINE MEDITATION

26. Matthew 18:3

27. St. Thérèse of Lisieux, *The Story of a Soul,* Double Day, 2001, p.179.

28. Bottaro, Gregory, *The Mindful Catholic: Finding God One Moment at a Time,* Beacon Publishing, 2018, p.3-4.

29. Bottaro, Gregory, *The Mindful Catholic: Finding God One Moment at a Time,* Beacon Publishing, 2018, p.29.

30. Bottaro, Gregory, *The Mindful Catholic: Finding God One Moment at a Time,* Beacon Publishing, 2018, p.16.

31. St. Thérèse of Lisieux, *The Story of a Soul,* Double Day, 2001, p. 179 and 222.

32. Bottaro, Gregory, *The Mindful Catholic: Finding God One Moment at a Time,* Beacon Publishing, 2018, p.32-33.

33. Bottaro, Gregory, *The Mindful Catholic: Finding God One Moment at a Time,* Beacon Publishing, 2018, p.69 and 87.

34. Bottaro, Gregory, *The Mindful Catholic: Finding God One Moment at a Time,* Beacon Publishing, 2018, p.27.

35. Bottaro, Gregory, *The Mindful Catholic: Finding God One Moment at a Time,* Beacon Publishing, 2018, p.92.

36. Bottaro, Gregory, *The Mindful Catholic: Finding God One Moment at a Time,* Beacon Publishing, 2018, p.33 and 94.

37. Bottaro, Gregory, *The Mindful Catholic: Finding God One Moment at a Time,* Beacon Publishing, 2018, p.39-40.

38. Bottaro, Gregory, *The Mindful Catholic: Finding God One Moment at a Time,* Beacon Publishing, 2018, p.101and 147.

39. Bottaro, Gregory, *The Mindful Catholic: Finding God One Moment at a Time,* Beacon Publishing, 2018, p.113 and 147.

40. Bottaro, Gregory, *The Mindful Catholic: Finding God One Moment at a Time,* Beacon Publishing, 2018, p.33.

41. Lewis, C.S. *The Screwtape Letters,* Harper One, 2015, Chapter 15.

42. Bottaro, Gregory, *The Mindful Catholic: Finding God One Moment at a Time,* Beacon Publishing, 2018, p.77.

43. Bottaro, Gregory, *The Mindful Catholic: Finding God One Moment at a Time,* Beacon Publishing, 2018, p.65.

44. Bottaro, Gregory, *The Mindful Catholic: Finding God One Moment at a Time,* Beacon Publishing, 2018, p.27 and 63.

22. LEAN IN

45. Barron, Robert. "*A Tale of Two Widows.*" Word on Fire. November 11, 2018.

46. 1 Kings 17:10

47. D'Elbée, Jean C.J., *I Believe in Love: A personal retreat based on the teachings of St. Thérèse of Lisieux,* Sophia Institute Press, 2001, p.18.

23. MISSION

48. de Caussade, Jean-Pierre. *Abandonment to Divine Providence,* Images Books, 2014, p. 23.

49. Luke 1:31

50. de Caussade, Jean-Pierre. *Abandonment to Divine Providence,* Images Books, 2014, p. 22.

51. Luke 10:41

24. YEAR SEVEN

52. St. Thérèse of Lisieux, *The Story of a Soul,* Double Day, 2001, p. 178.

53. Chesterton G.K, Orthodoxy.

54. St. John Paul II, Apostolic Journey to the Far East and Oceania, November 30, 1986.

26. DEAR DAUGHTER

55. 2 Corinthians 6:10

This story was made possible by:

- The inspiration and power of the Holy Spirit,
- My children and their capacity to inspire wonder and bravery,
- My husband, without whom this story would not have been possible,
- My mom and cheerleader and my dad and confidence jolt,
- The many women who taught me that my story mattered and that chaos and creativity can coexist,
- Kathie Brown, the architect of education I cherish as well as a patient and proficient editor,
- Ken McConnellogue, whose pro insights brought my story to the next level,
- Steve Kuhn, my ace designer,
- And you—thank you for reading!

Made in the USA
Monee, IL
23 October 2023

45043775R00111